Timaeus

Plato

Timaeus

Translated,
with Introduction, by
DONALD J. ZEYL

Hackett Publishing Company
Indianapolis/Cambridge

06 05 04 03 02 01 00   1 2 3 4 5 6 7 8

For further information, please address:

Hackett Publishing Company, Inc.
P.O. Box 44937
Indianapolis, IN 46244-0937

www.hackettpublishing.com

Cover design by Listenberger Design & Associates

Interior design by Abigail Coyle

Library of Congress Cataloging-in-Publication Data

Plato.
[Timaeus. English]
Timaeus / Plato ; translated, with introduction by Donald J. Zeyl.
p. cm.
Includes bibliographical references.
ISBN 0-87220-447-2 (alk. paper)—ISBN 0-87220-446-4 (pbk. : alk. paper)
1. Cosmology.   I. Zeyl, Donald J., 1944–   II. Title.
B387.A5 Z4913 2000
113—dc21   99-059574

The paper used in this publication meets the minimum standard
requirements of American National Standard for Information Sciences—
Permanence of Paper for Printed Materials, ANSI Z39.48-1984.

For Jonathan and Rochelle
and
Jennifer

CONTENTS

FOREWORD

Translating Plato's *Timaeus* presents a formidable challenge. The formal and elevated style of Timaeus' discourse and its technical subject matter and vocabulary are unlike those of any other passage of comparable length in the Platonic corpus. Both of these features of Plato's prose in this dialogue account for a complexity of thought and expression that is not easily grasped, let alone conveyed in another language. In producing this translation I have striven to understand and represent in English as closely as possible what Plato intended his readers to grasp. I can only hope that I have had some measure of success. I have been the fortunate beneficiary of a long tradition of superb scholarship on the *Timaeus*. In particular, I have benefited from the commentary by A. E. Taylor [39][1] and the translation and running commentary by F. M. Cornford [14]. These works remain indispensable to a serious study of the dialogue, and whenever I have chosen to reject their translations or interpretations—as I frequently believed I had reason to do—it has not been without utmost consideration. A vast quantity of scholarship on the *Timaeus*—variously philological, philosophical, and scientific—has been produced in the last two-thirds of the 20th century and has challenged and revised long-standing orthodoxies and set new directions. In preparing this new translation and the introduction that precedes it I wish to reflect much of this more recent work.

The lengthy introductory essay I provide is intended to do more than acquaint readers with the *Timaeus* itself. It is intended also as an introduction to the controversies about the interpretation of the dialogue—some almost as old as the work itself, but most as recent as the last half century. I consider in some detail the hoary question of whether the *Timaeus* is meant to be read literally or metaphorically, as well as the issue (by comparison, recent) of whether it should be placed in the "middle" group of Platonic dialogues or should keep its traditional place within the "late" dialogues. My own views on these matters will become apparent; I hope I have done justice to opposing views. As I go

---

1. Bracketed numbers indicate entries in the Select Bibliography, pp. 89–94.

on to discuss the text, section by section, I take note of interpretive issues and the secondary literature that discusses them, sometimes raising interpretive questions of my own. These issues will generally not be clear or relevant to the reader unless they are studied in conjunction with the corresponding parts of the *Timaeus* itself, and readers will be well advised to defer their reading of these parts of the Introduction until they come to those corresponding parts of the dialogue. Finally, the last half of the discourse—from about 58c on—has generated much less interpretive debate than its first half, though it is no less technical and is in places relatively obscure. My commentary accordingly is meant to summarize and clarify what otherwise might remain obscure. It goes without saying that a reading of these summaries is no substitute for a close study of the text itself.

The notes to the translation report readings of the text I have followed that vary from those adopted by J. Burnet in his edition of Plato's works in the *Oxford Classical Texts* (*OCT*) series.[2] In addition, I have included in the notes—sometimes at considerable length—explanatory material I believe to be necessary or appropriate for understanding the passage annotated. Interpretive discussion is left to the Introduction. In the Analytical Table of Contents, the Introduction, and the notes to the translation, I give not only the Stephanus page and section numbers, but also the line numbering, for the benefit of any readers who wish to consult the Greek text. It should be noted that the line numbering given does not necessarily correspond to the line sequence of the translation.

Both the translation and the Introduction have benefited from the critical and constructive scrutiny of several scholars. C. D. C. Reeve gave helpful feedback on the translation of the Prologue to the Discourse. T. M. Robinson read an early draft of the entire translation. He drew my attention to several alternative readings of the text in various places (see [90] and [91] of the Select Bibliography) and suggested many appropriate changes. John Cooper (as an editor of *Plato: Complete Works* [13], in which the translation has previously appeared) proposed numerous changes that challenged my tendency to excessive literalism. His critique has brought about the most improvement in the translation. An anonymous reader for the publisher proposed helpful changes in an early and incomplete draft of the Introduction. John Cooper again

2. J. Burnet, *Platonis Opera*, vol. 4. Oxford: Clarendon Press, 1902.

read the entire Introduction and helped to improve it. I am deeply grateful to each of these scholars. I have not always followed their advice, no doubt often to my detriment, and take full responsibility for the remaining deficiencies.

INTRODUCTION

The *Timaeus* is Plato's creation story. According to that story, a divine craftsman or demiurge imposed order and beauty upon a preexisting chaos to fashion our world in the likeness of an eternal model. Guided both by his own nature as a supremely excellent deity and by the excellence of his model, the world he created is a living, intelligent organism that magnificently displays mathematical order and proportion in both its soul and its body, in its larger structure as well as in the constitution of its smallest parts.

Why should we take such a story seriously? Has not the prevailing naturalism in modern science since the 17th century made creation stories obsolete, perhaps of some historical interest but irrelevant to a contemporary scientific understanding of the universe and of ourselves? The answer to this question today is no longer an unqualified yes. The widespread acceptance of Big Bang cosmology has given new life to the question of what, if anything, caused the Big Bang to occur—thus giving room to the idea that the universe might have been created. And the observation that the fundamental constants underlying the physics of the universe are so finely tuned and integrated as to give the appearance of design—the so-called Anthropic Principle—has revived in some minds the possibility (and in others the specter) of a divine creator. The mere fact that at the turn of the millennium these questions are once again hotly debated by scientists and philosophers is testimony to the continuing appeal of seeing the world as the handiwork of an intelligent mind.

Even if we are not inclined to follow Plato in the belief that the world has been divinely created, we may still be fascinated by other aspects of his story. Plato describes that story as an *eikōs logos* or *mythos*, a "likely account" (or "likely story"), and we wonder what he has in mind by that description. To what extent is his story properly a part of the history of science? How does it connect with the project of "inquiry into nature" (*peri phuseōs historia*), a project in which many of his predecessors and contemporaries were actively engaged? How does Plato shed light on their project, and how does their work illuminate the *Timaeus*? Given that the vehicle of Plato's account is a creation "myth," to what extent can or should it be "demythologized"? Does Plato take his story of the beginning of the world literally? If so, can it be related to contemporary Big Bang theory?[1] What doctrines about the nature of space and matter are to be found in the physics of the dialogue? On what basis does Plato link knowledge of the mathematical structure of the world with the good life? And what about the literary aspects of the work? How is its content related to its literary form? What is the role of the Atlantis myth that precedes the discourse? Is it a literary invention of Plato's? If so, what is its purpose, and how does it relate to the creation story? These and other questions are prompted by a reading of the *Timaeus* and testify to its contemporary interest and importance.

From late antiquity onward, throughout the Middle Ages and well into modern times, the *Timaeus* enjoyed a position of preeminence among Plato's works. Most widely studied and most influential of the dialogues—during the Middle Ages it was virtually the only work of Plato's that had been translated into Latin[2]—it was regarded as the definitive expression of his philosophy.[3] The splendid vision of a mathematically ordered world modeled after the eternal, paradigmatic Forms—a work of art conceived and executed by a supremely wise and good deity—was received as the fitting climax of Plato's transcendental philosophy and commended itself to generations of theologians of the early Christian era as philosophical corroboration of their own creation theologies.[4] Although Plato's influence as a whole declined during the later Middle Ages, the *Timaeus* retained its preeminence among Plato's dialogues well into the 19th century, when it was eclipsed by the *Republic*.

In the 20th century the fortunes of the *Timaeus* have been mixed. A. E. Taylor's erudite commentary on the text,[5] masterly

---

1. For a speculative recent account of such a relationship, see Brisson and Meyerstein [7].

2. Cicero's (106–43 B.C.E.) translation of the *Timaeus* survives only in fragments. A more substantial translation and commentary, by Calcidius (fl. c. 350 C.E.), is extant only to 53c [8]. Plutarch's (c. 45–125 C.E.) *On the Generation of the World Soul in the Timaeus* is a source for ancient controversies about the dialogue [33], and Proclus (412–85 C.E.) provides ample commentary, extant only as far as 44d [36].

3. See Prior [35], pp. 176–78.

4. For an excellent study of Christian appropriations of the *Timaeus*, see Pelikan [31].

5. Taylor [39].

in its detail, was flawed by the author's assumption that the dialogue's cosmological, psychological, and physiological doctrines were not Plato's own, but an amalgam of fifth-century Pythagorean mathematics and Empedoclean physics. Nine years later, in 1937, Taylor's view was effectively rebutted by F. M. Cornford in his translation of and commentary on the dialogue.[6] By mid-century, interest in the *Timaeus* had declined, particularly in the English-speaking world, where, in the wake of the antimetaphysical turn of Logical Positivism, the methods of "linguistic analysis" predominated. Plato's theory of Forms came to be seen as a tissue of linguistic confusions, of which Plato began to disabuse himself only in his later period, in dialogues like the *Parmenides, Theaetetus,* and *Sophist.* These three were read as "critical" exploratory essays in philosophical logic and the philosophy of language, areas in which figures such as Frege, Russell, and Wittgenstein had done groundbreaking work during the last quarter of the 19th and first half of the 20th century. This revisionist approach to Plato's development had implications for the *Timaeus.* Since its cosmology was undeniably based upon the metaphysics of the theory of Forms and lacked the features of the more mature "critical" dialogues, it was regarded as lacking any serious philosophical significance.[7] In addition, since the work, after an introductory conversation, consists of a monologue from which the give-and-take of discussion is entirely absent, it was in any case unsuitable for those pedagogical purposes so beautifully achieved by most of Plato's other dialogues.

In recent years, the *Timaeus* has received renewed interest, owing in part to the emergence of a more tolerant view of metaphysics and hence of the metaphysical theories of the philosophers of the past. The metaphysics of Plato's middle period, for example, is now generally appreciated as a serious and largely coherent (whether mistaken or not) attempt to answer genuine and important questions about the nature of knowledge and of reality.[8] Fresh examinations of crucial texts have yielded accounts of Plato's development that challenge the revisionist paradigm[9] and that allow the *Timaeus* to be taken seriously as philosophy.

---

6. Cornford [14]; see pp. vi–ix.

7. Many who shared this view of the dialogue came to be persuaded that the *Timaeus* was not a late dialogue at all, but preceded the *Parmenides* and *Theaetetus* in order of composition. See below, pp. xvi–xx.

8. See White [101], Mueller [77].

9. See, for example, Prior [35].

The Place of the *Timaeus* in the Order of Plato's Dialogues

Possibly the most far-reaching controversy in Platonic scholarship since the mid-20th century concerns the position of the *Timaeus* in the order of Plato's dialogues. Since this controversy is still widely referred to in the current literature, I shall discuss it at some length.

As noted earlier, from antiquity onward the dialogue enjoyed an unchallenged reputation as the crowning work of Plato's maturity. In consequence, it tended to be regarded as among the last of Plato's written works. A number of diverse studies of changes in Plato's style begun in the last third of the 19th century (more on these below) confirmed the tradition: the *Timaeus* and its sequel, the *Critias,* were universally taken to have been written late in Plato's life.

That orthodoxy was vigorously challenged in 1953 in a much discussed and widely influential article by G. E. L. Owen,[10] who called into question the reliability or applicability of the results of "stylometric" analysis which had certified the orthodoxy. Owen charged that insofar as these results appear to require placing the *Timaeus* after, rather than before, dialogues such as the *Parmenides* and *Theaetetus,* they import intolerable "paradoxes" into an account of Plato's philosophical development. To eliminate these paradoxes, Owen proposed reassigning the *Timaeus* to an earlier chronological position, after the *Republic* and before the *Parmenides* and *Theaetetus*—dialogues that he and others termed "critical" and that in his view ushered in a less muddled and more sophisticated phase of Plato's philosophical activity. Owen's case won a considerable following, especially among British scholars, but from the start it has been the subject of sometimes acrimonious debate. The context of the matters at issue may be described as follows.

It is customary to divide the corpus of the Platonic dialogues into three major groups.[11] Within which of these groups, and at

---

10. Owen [81].

11. A widely accepted ordering of the dialogues divides them into three major groups, with a subdivision within the first and an assignment of the *Meno* to a "transitional" position between the first and the second. (I leave aside the *Timaeus* and *Critias.*) I. Early Dialogues: (a) earlier group (in alphabetical order): *Apology, Charmides, Crito, Euthyphro, Gorgias, Hippias Minor, Ion, Laches,* and *Protagoras*; (b)

what place within the chosen group, are we to place the *Timaeus* and *Critias*? And what are the consequences of placing these dialogues within one group or at one place rather than another? The tradition that placed the two works in the group of late dialogues, followed only by the *Laws* and possibly the *Philebus*,[12] seemed vindicated by painstaking stylometric studies that sought to put an end to the subjectivity which had produced an array of diverse accounts of the order of Plato's dialogues. In detecting and subjecting to careful analysis a variety of subtle changes in Plato's style over the course of his literary lifetime, the stylometrists wanted to find a firm and objective basis for a chronological ordering of his works.[13] It was reasonably assumed that those dialogues which shared various clusters of stylistic characteristics could be grouped together chronologically, even if an order within any of these groups might be difficult, or impossible, to determine. Taking as their benchmark the lateness of the *Laws*,[14] they assumed, again reasonably, that those dialogues which are most similar to the *Laws* in the relevant stylistic characteristics belong to the last period of Plato's life. Hence those dialogues that differ markedly in style from the dialogues within this group are presumed to have been written earlier.[15]

Five features of Plato's style could be seen to have undergone either a sudden or a gradual change over the course of his writing,

---

later group (in alphabetical order): *Euthydemus* (?), *Hippias Major, Lysis, Menexenus,* and *Republic I.* [Transitional: *Meno.*] II. Middle Dialogues (in a plausible order): *Cratylus* (?), *Phaedo, Symposium, Republic, Parmenides, Theaetetus,* and *Phaedrus.* III. Late Dialogues: *Sophist, Statesman* (often named *Politicus*), *Philebus,* and *Laws.* See Kraut [67], pp. 5, 9, and [68], pp. 388–89. As indicated, there is no consensus about the placing of the *Euthydemus* and *Cratylus.* For a salutary reminder of the limitations of this sort of ordering, see J. Cooper in [13], pp. xii–xviii.

12. For the tradition, see Prior [35], pp. 168–78. More recent stylometric studies now include the *Sophist* and *Statesman* among the dialogues that follow the *Timaeus.* See n. 23 below and text *ad loc.*

13. The major stylistic studies are presented and extensively discussed in Brandwood [5] and more briefly in [47]. See also Young [104].

14. Aristotle reports (*Politics* II.6, 1264b24–27) that the *Laws* was written after the *Republic,* a statement repeated by other ancient authorities (Diogenes Laertius III.37; Olympiodorus, *Prol.* VI.24), together with the report that it was left unrevised on wax tablets at the time of Plato's death (Olympiodorus, ibid.).

15. Within the large group of dialogues not similar to the *Laws* two subgroups could be discerned, again, on the basis of stylistical similarities and differences. The ordering of those two groups was determined, again, by degree of similarity to the *Laws* group. See Brandwood [47].

including (1) his use of technical terminology; (2) his preference for one synonymous expression over another; (3) his choice of reply formulae in dialogic contexts; (4) his readiness to avoid "hiatus," that is, the juxtaposition of two words of which the first ends, and the second begins, with a vowel; and (5) his choice of prose rhythm, in particular of the clausula, the final four or five syllables of a sentence or colon. The changes in Plato's style that an investigation into these features revealed were of two kinds: an earlier one, involving features 1, 2, and 3, which was slow and gradual and in which the changes are uneven and probably unconscious; and a later one, involving features 4 and 5, which was sudden and rapid, and no doubt deliberate.[16]

The stylometric studies available to Owen had uniformly placed the *Timaeus* and *Critias* within a distinct group that included the *Sophist, Statesman, Philebus*, and *Laws*. Owen challenged the evidence in various ways.[17] Principally, he charged that the methods and assumptions of the stylometrists are unreliable, that the unique subject matter and hence the abundance of technical vocabulary of the *Timaeus* rules out comparison with other dialogues, and that the "*tour de force* of style" in the bulk of the work— Timaeus' uninterrupted discourse—explains its high incidence of hiatus avoidance (feature 4 above). Plato, Owen speculated, might have experimented with hiatus avoidance in the formal speech of the *Timaeus,* only to drop the convention in the dialogues that immediately followed (including the *Parmenides* and *Theaetetus*), then to readopt the convention permanently for the remainder of his literary output (the dialogues *Sophist, Statesman, Philebus,* and *Laws*). On the other hand, Owen claimed to find in earlier studies of the rhythms of Plato's clausulae (feature 5 above) support for his earlier dating.

The paradoxes that, according to Owen, the traditional position of the *Timaeus* imports into the interpretation of Plato's philosophy were primarily two. First, the *Parmenides* attacks a feature of the theory of Forms that had been an essential aspect of it in the "precritical" dialogues, namely, its paradeigmatism: sensible particulars are standardly conceived in those dialogues as *copies* of the various Forms in which they participate. The second regress

---

16. See Brandwood [5], p. 249.

17. See Owen [81], pp. 314–18. Owen's objections are conveniently enumerated in Prior [35], pp. 182–83.

argument of the *Parmenides* (132d–33a) appears to undermine the coherence of this conception by arguing that copies and originals must be like each other, and that if any two or more things are like each other, they are so by virtue of a Form "over" them all. So if a given sensible particular is like a Form in respect of being F, there must be a second Form of F "over" them both. According to Owen, in the *Parmenides* Plato came to understand that it is a mistake to conceive of sensibles as likenesses of Forms. Yet in the *Timaeus* sensible particulars are conceived of in just that way.

Second, the terms of the distinction between "being" and "becoming," familiar from the *Republic*, are presented in the *Timaeus* as mutually exclusive: that which has being has no becoming, and that which becomes has no being (27d6–28a2). But according to Owen, as early as the *Theaetetus* this way of conceiving the distinction comes under fire; in that dialogue Plato argues that any subject that only "becomes" without "being" anything (either by retaining a certain quality over time or occupying a certain place over time) cannot be referred to or described, that is, it cannot be talked about at all (182c–183b), so that the notion of something becoming without being (anything) is incoherent. In admittedly late dialogues where the being/becoming distinction reappears, the *Sophist* (248a–249b) and *Philebus* (26d8, 27b8–9, 54a–d), the terms of the distinction are no longer mutually exclusive.[18]

Owen sought to support his overall argument for an earlier date of the *Timaeus* by three further arguments, none of which, however, is as fundamental to the interpretation of Plato's philosophy as the two just discussed.[19] At best, these arguments show that the *Timaeus* precedes the *Sophist* and *Statesman*. Even if Owen is correct, these arguments do nothing to show that the *Timaeus* is a middle dialogue that precedes the *Parmenides* and *Theaetetus*.

Owen's case for a "middle period" *Timaeus* has been vigorously disputed over the years. Three years after its publication,

---

18. Owen also included the *Parmenides* among the dialogues in which the mutual exclusivity is presumably denied (at *Parm.* 163d1–2).

19. He also argued (1) that Eudoxus' theory of planetary motion was unknown to Plato when he wrote the *Timaeus* but known to him by the time he wrote the *Laws* (on this see below, pp. xlviii–xlix); (2) that a prior acquaintance with the *Sophist* is not presupposed in the psychogony of *Tim.* 35a; and (3) that the political structure at *Tim.* 17c–19a (a reprise of the *Republic*) is at odds with that proposed in the *Statesman*, traditionally assumed to be earlier than the *Timaeus*.

H. F. Cherniss launched a broadside attack on it, challenging (1) Owen's treatment of the stylometric evidence, (2) his interpretation of Plato's paradeigmatism and the *Parmenides* regress, and (3) his account of the being/becoming distinction in the later dialogues.[20] Although it is far from true that anything approaching unanimity in favor of the traditional place of the *Timaeus* has emerged, it is fair to say in retrospect that Owen's case is far less compelling than it seemed to many when it was first presented.[21] To begin with, Owen's central stylometric arguments have been effectively controverted. The high degree of hiatus avoidance which the *Timaeus* shares with the four admittedly late dialogues has been reestablished as a firm indication of its lateness, not to be explained away by the dialogue's special character,[22] and while the clausulae criterion on which Owen relied might justify placing the *Timaeus* before the *Sophist* and *Statesman*, it falls far short of justifying its placement, crucial for Owen's case, before the *Parmenides* and *Theaetetus*.[23] Second, a spate of more recent studies of the development of Plato's metaphysics has reassessed the arguments of the *Parmenides* and *Theaetetus* which Owen claimed were in conflict with the metaphysics of the *Timaeus*, as well as that metaphysics itself, and, despite their sometimes widely divergent accounts, these studies have shown that the relevant arguments of these dialogues need not be interpreted as Owen has interpreted them—indeed, that they should not be so interpreted.[24]

The Creation Story: Literal or Metaphorical?

A fundamental question that immediately confronts any reader of the *Timaeus* concerns the character of Plato's account. Plato offers an elaborate creation story in which a divine craftsman, guided by his ideas of what is most beautiful and best, constructs

---

20. Cherniss [49].

21. For subsequent criticism of Owen (sometimes including criticisms of Cherniss's rebuttal), see Prior [35], pp. 168–93; Fine [55], pp. 374–79; and particularly Mueller [77], pp. 8–20, whose review of the stylistic evidence is especially valuable.

22. See Prior [35], pp. 185–87.

23. It is primarily on the basis of this criterion that Brandwood places the *Timaeus* and *Critias* before the *Sophist* and *Statesman*. See Brandwood [5], p. 250, and [47], pp. 113–14.

24. See, for example, Waterlow [100], Patterson [30], and Prior [35].

out of an unordered and erratic chaos a unique world conceived as a psychophysical organism, an everlasting "living thing." Are we to understand this story literally, as a step-by-step creative process in which, at the beginning of time, the craftsman god actually *created* the world? Or is the story an extended metaphor, artfully depicting as a deliberate creative process those fundamental principles that in Plato's view underlie an eternally existing physical cosmos? Or, perhaps, is it that same metaphorical story told with an interest in the principles fundamental to the existing cosmos but with no interest in whether or not it is eternal? The controversy between a "literal" and a "metaphorical" reading of the *Timaeus* is almost as old as the dialogue itself. Aristotle, for example, clearly interpreted the creation account literally when he attacked the view that time has a beginning, a view he attributed to Plato, obviously on the basis of the *Timaeus*.[25] On the other hand Xenocrates—Aristotle's contemporary and a fellow member of Plato's Academy—perhaps in defense against such attacks, maintained that the account was metaphorical, and that the creation "story" is a mere pedagogical device.[26] The Neoplatonist Proclus (412–85 C.E.) reports that Xenocrates' student and successor Crantor perpetuated the metaphorical view, which appears to have been the dominant one among subsequent generations of Platonists down to the time of Plotinus (204/5–70 C.E.), though the literal view was also maintained by at least two eminent Platonists of the first and second centuries C.E., Plutarch and Atticus.[27] The controversy lives on in the 20th century: the metaphorical view has been championed by scholars such as Taylor, Cornford, Cherniss, and Tarán,[28] while the literal view counts Vlastos, Hackforth, Sorabji, Robinson, and others among its defenders.[29]

Those who prefer the metaphorical reading of the creation account have been motivated primarily by what they perceive to be the following difficulties presented by a literal reading.

---

25. For the attribution and the attack, see *Physics* 251b14–26. Compare *Timaeus* 38b6: "Time came to be together with the universe. . . ."

26. Aristotle, *On the Heavens* 279b32–280a1. The allusion is to Xenocrates, third head of the Academy and a contemporary of Aristotle.

27. For recent discussion of various Neoplatonic interpretations of Plato's cosmogony, see Phillips [86].

28. Taylor [39], pp. 66–70; Cornford [14], pp. 24–32, 34–39; Cherniss [11], pp. 392–457 and notes; Tarán [94].

29. Vlastos [95] and [96]; Hackforth [63]; Sorabji [38], pp. 272–75; Robinson [89].

(1) Plato presents his story under certain qualifications, particularly the one that his account is merely a "likely account" (*eikōs logos*), or even "likely story" (*"eikōs mythos,"* 29d2). We are not, he tells us, to expect accounts that are "completely and perfectly consistent and accurate" (29c5–7). This is an indication that the story is an extended metaphor and should not be understood literally. Moreover, Plato frequently injects comments throughout the dialogue that his creation story should not be pressed.

(2) Certain elements in the story are clearly mythical and produce absurdities if read literally. We obviously should not be asking, for example, what the bowl in which the soul mixture was prepared was made of (41d), or how there can be portions of Being, Sameness, and Difference and how they can be mixed together and divided mathematically (35a *ff.*). Moreover, there seems to be no clear line between what is to be taken literally and what is to be understood metaphorically. In consequence, the figure of a divine craftsman is best understood as a symbol and is not meant to represent a distinct reality in Plato's scheme; he is reducible to one of the other factors in Plato's account, such as the world soul[30] (or at least the intelligence of the world soul[31]), or the Forms[32] or a particular Form—perhaps the Form of the Good[33] or the Form of Intelligence.[34]

(3) Plato presents the craftsman as constructing a cosmos out of a previously existing chaotic condition. If we take this "precosmos" literally, then we commit ourselves to the existence of time prior to the generation of the cosmos or, more pointedly, prior to the generation of time itself, which is obviously absurd.

(4) In the *Timaeus,* Plato represents the world soul, and individual souls, as having been created. Elsewhere, for example in the *Phaedrus* (245c–e), he holds that the soul is uncreated. This is an intolerable contradiction, which may be resolved by reading the "creation" of soul metaphorically.

(5) Elsewhere, for example, in the *Phaedrus* and *Laws*, Plato holds that the soul is the origin of all motion. In the *Timaeus,* how-

---

30. Archer-Hind [4], p. 39.
31. Cornford [14], pp. 38–39.
32. DeVogel [15], pp. 194–209, and [16], p. 73; Perl [85].
33. Hampton [23], p. 909.
34. Menn [27].

ever, there is motion not originated by soul: the erratic motion of the Receptacle and its contents in the precosmos. This contradiction, too, can be resolved if the situation in the precosmos is not understood literally.

In general, proponents of a metaphorical interpretation tend to argue that a literal reading produces contradictions and absurdities in Plato's philosophy, both within the *Timaeus* and between the *Timaeus* and other dialogues—contradictions of which a thinker of Plato's stature would not have been unaware and which he would not have tolerated. Since these contradictions cease to matter if the *Timaeus* is read metaphorically, we should suppose that Plato intended the creation account of the *Timaeus* to be read in this way.

To these arguments the proponents of a literal interpretation make the following replies.

(1) Plato's qualifications, particularly his characterization of the account as "likely," afford no license to demythologize.[35] On the contrary, since Plato insists that the account is "no less likely than any" (29c7–8), the availability of some other, more likely, account is precluded. But any demythologized version of the account (the "real" story "behind" the myth) would surely be more likely than the story Plato actually tells. Moreover, throughout the dialogue Plato explicitly identifies for us those parts of his account which should not be pressed for literal accuracy.[36] These markers suggest, in their view, that the overall account is meant to be taken literally.

(2) Many mythical elements in the dialogue can be acknowledged, but the differences between the *Timaeus* story and the myths in other Platonic dialogues (the *Gorgias, Phaedo, Republic, Phaedrus,* and *Statesman*), which clearly are metaphorical, are unmistakable.[37] Nor can the craftsman be reduced to the world soul (or mind), to the Forms or to any particular Form. Plato is quite prepared to speak of a "craftsman of the universe" elsewhere, in contexts that are clearly free of mythology.[38] The craftsman may indeed be a personifi-

---

35. Vlastos [95], p. 382; Hackforth [63], p. 19; Robinson [89], p. 111.
36. See, for example, 34c2–4, 61c4–d4.
37. See Vlastos [95], pp. 380–83.
38. *Rep.* 530a6; cf. 507c6–7.

cation, namely, of that Intellect (*nous*) which is described in
the *Philebus* (23c–30e) as the "cause of the mixture" of limit
(*peras*) and the unlimited (*apeiron*). But he cannot be reduced
or demythologized out of the *Timaeus* without distortion.[39]

(3) The apparent problem of a "time before time" can also be
solved. The time that "came to be together with the universe"
is not duration as such, but duration that is measurable by the
revolutions "according to number" (38d6) of the sun, moon,
planets, and fixed stars around the earth. What preceded the
advent of this enumerable and divisible time was precosmic
time: unmeasured temporal flow, characterized merely by
succession, a "trace" of ordered time.[40]

(4) It is true that the *Timaeus'* doctrine of the creation of soul
contradicts the claim of the *Phaedrus* that soul is ungenerated.
But if it is the case, as almost all scholars believe, that the
Phaedrus antedates the *Timaeus*, then what we may have here
is simply a change of mind on Plato's part. This impression
is confirmed in the *Laws*, which is reasonably presumed to
be Plato's latest work,[41] where soul is described in a clearly
nonmythological context as "the first *genesis*" (896a6, 899c7)
and "eldest of the things that partake of generation" (*gonē*,
967d6–7). If it is clear that Plato changed his mind between
the *Phaedrus* and the *Laws*, then the *Timaeus* may well be read
as making that change a matter of record.[42]

(5) It is conceded that the erratic motions of the Receptacle and
its contents cannot plausibly be attributed to soul. There is
no textual evidence for an irrational (part of the) world soul
animating the precosmos. The precosmic movements are due
not to the presence of soul, but to the *absence* of the regulative
function of soul. These motions are inherent in the Receptacle
and the "raw material" out of which the cosmos was made,
and continue to persist in it to the extent that nonuniformity
(*anomalotēs*, 57e) persists. Soul is the origin of all *purposive* and
orderly motion, motion that is intelligible and predictable. The

---

39. See Robinson [89], pp. 113–15.

40. For a developed version of this view, see Vlastos [96], pp. 409–14. Compare
the "traces" of the elements that existed in the precosmos (53b2).

41. I do not mean to rule out the possibility that the *Laws* may have been written
over a long period of time, during which several shorter works may have been
written as well.

42. See Vlastos [96], pp. 414–15.

inherent convulsions of the Receptacle and its contents are erratic, hence unintelligible and unpredictable. The motion that the *Phaedrus* and *Laws* passages have in view is only of the intelligible kind.

In addition to these responses, defenders of a literal reading believe that they have one argument in their favor which trumps the objections against their position: at 28b6–7 Timaeus asks whether the world has always existed or whether it has come to be. He answers unhesitatingly that "it has come to be" (*gegonen*). What, they claim, could be a clearer signal of Plato's belief in the world's temporal beginning than that?

Introductory Conversation: 17a–27d

As the dialogue begins, we find Socrates meeting with three friends, the Athenian Critias and two visitors from the western Greek world, Timaeus and Hermocrates. They have gathered for a second day to exchange speeches in celebration of the goddess Athena, patron deity of Athens, whose festival, the Panathenaea, is current being celebrated.[43] Socrates has already contributed his speech on the previous day and now eagerly awaits the gift of his friends' speeches in exchange for his.

Socrates hardly needs an introduction. He is the Athenian philosopher (469–399 B.C.E.) who profoundly influenced Plato and is well known as the primary interlocutor in all but a few of Plato's dialogues. But who are the other three participants?[44] Critias, too, is an Athenian, very likely the grandfather of the Critias who later became one of the Thirty Tyrants, and Plato's own great-grandfather. He is a namesake of his own grandfather, eighty years his senior and Solon's friend (20e–21d). Hermocrates is a citizen of Syracuse, in Sicily, and probably the military leader who defeated the Athenian expedition against Sicily in 415–13 B.C.E. (see Thucydides IV.58 and VI.72). About Timaeus, the main speaker of the dialogue, we know nothing outside of the dialogue. He purportedly comes from Locri, a city in southern Italy "under the rule of excellent laws" (20a2) where he has held all the magis-

---

43. The Panathenaea was celebrated every year, during Hekatombaion (roughly August). Every four years the Great Panathenaea, a more elaborate festival, was celebrated. It is not indicated whether the current festival was a Great Panathenaea.

44. It is anybody's guess why a *fifth* participant, present "yesterday" but absent "today," is mentioned.

tracies. He participates in the exchange of speeches as the "expert in astronomy" (27a3–4). It is probable that he is fictional, Plato's own invention (a treatise, the *Timaeus Locrus*, bears his name, but that document is a first-century forgery[45]). It would suit Plato's purpose to present the array of ideas of the *Timaeus* by means of a fictional character: to put them into the mouth of Socrates would be to violate history,[46] and to attribute them to an actual contemporary or recent figure would call into question Plato's originality.[47]

Before proceeding to give their own speeches, Socrates' friends request him to rehearse the main points of the speech he has given on the previous day. Socrates reminds them that its subject was that of the "best political structure" cities should have, and he proceeds to sum up the main features of that structure. The class of guardians—those charged with maintaining and protecting the city and its constitution—are to be separated off from the other classes. The guardians alone have natures suitable to their task, "at once spirited and philosophical," displayed in behavior appropriate to foreigners and fellow citizens alike. They are to be given both physical (*gymnastikē*) and cultural (*mousikē*) training and may not own property. They are to be remunerated modestly, share in a common way of life, and pursue excellence. All the occupations of guardianship should be shared by both men and women, and spouses and children are to be held in common. Procreative liaisons would be arranged for eugenic purposes by the rulers by means of a rigged lottery, and the progress of the children produced by these liaisons closely monitored (17c–19a).

To any reader of the *Republic* all of this will sound like a reprise of much of that dialogue, and the question about the relationship between the dramatic dates of the *Republic* and *Timaeus* has been much discussed. Some have assumed that Socrates' speech of "yesterday" is in fact the whole *Republic*, itself a narration of a

---

45. See Taylor [39], pp. 655–64.

46. Aristotle reports (*Met.* 987b1–2) that Socrates confined his philosophical inquiries to matters of conduct, not "nature as a whole." In the *Apology* (19b–c), Socrates disclaims ever having engaged in physical inquiry. Plato's representation of Socrates in the *Phaedo* as having had an early interest in natural science is rejected by most scholars as historically inaccurate; in any case, even if we take the *Phaedo* passage as historically accurate, Socrates says he abandoned this interest because he became disenchanted with it.

47. I am assuming that Taylor's hypothesis that the doctrines of the *Timaeus* are *not* Plato's own but an amalgam of Pythagorean and Empedoclean theorizing of the late fifth century (see above, p. xv) has been discredited.

discussion of the day before (*Rep.* 327a1). If so, the dramatic dates of the dialogues are but two days apart.[48] There is, however, no reason to assume that "yesterday's speech" is in fact the narration of the *Republic*, and good reason to assume that it is not. Far from summarizing the *Republic* as a whole, Socrates' outline fails even to summarize the political constitution of that dialogue. The subdivision of the guardian class into rulers and auxiliaries, and the climax of the *Republic*'s political structure, the philosopher-king, are entirely absent. And yet Socrates and his interlocutors agree that no major point has been left out of the summary (19a7–b2). We should probably conclude that Plato wants to remind his readers of the political theory of the *Republic*, or at least some aspects of it, without intending them to draw any conclusion about the chronological, or even dramatic, proximity of these works.

Socrates' request is for a speech that will show off in action the city thus organized, and display its distinctive qualities and virtues. It is in response to this request that Critias proposes the tale of Atlantis, a story passed down to him by his aged grandfather and namesake. This tale will meet Socrates' requirements: it is the account of primeval Athens, a city organized on the principles developed in Socrates' previous speech, and, moreover, a city that has distinguished itself in action. This city single-handedly defeated some nine thousand years before the invading forces of Atlantis, a massive imperial power situated on an island in the Atlantic Ocean near the entrance to the Mediterranean Sea.

What is the basis of the Atlantis story? We have no account of anything like it from any other ancient writer. Is Plato refashioning an existing Greek mythological story or is he inventing one? Presumably, if there was an existing story of this sort, it would represent some actual event or series of events from the prehistoric past. If, on the other hand, it is a Platonic invention, what would motivate Plato to write it? The *Critias* as we have it (it breaks off in mid-sentence) is devoted entirely to a description of prehistoric Athens and Attica, and the island of Atlantis, and it was certainly intended to present an account of the Athenian victory over Atlantis (27a–b). Further, why does Plato have Critias insist on its truth (20d8, 26c7–d1, 26e4–5; cf. 21a5)? These questions have generated

---

48. So Taylor [39], p. 46, following Archer-Hind [4], pp. 54–55, and many commentators going back to Proclus. For criticism see Cornford [14], pp. 4 and 5. Cornford points out that it is very unlikely that the festival of Bendis, the dramatic setting of the *Republic*, would have preceded the Panathenaea by a mere two days.

much discussion, not to say controversy.[49] A more apposite question for our purposes is this: Why should Plato preface his cosmological discourse with this story, which, whether factual or fictitious, seems totally irrelevant to it?[50]

Plato seems to have intended the *Timaeus* to serve as the first member of a projected trilogy, to be followed by the *Critias* and, we may suppose, by the *Hermocrates*.[51] We are not told anywhere what the subject of the last of these dialogues was to be,[52] but it seems clear enough from the first ten pages of the *Timaeus* that the story of the defeat of Atlantis by ancient Athens was to have been the centerpiece of the trilogy, to which the cosmological account of the *Timaeus* is itself but a prelude (27a). Whatever Plato's reasons were for abandoning the trilogy—leaving the *Critias* unfinished—it is safe to assume that as he began the *Timaeus*, he intended its prologue to serve as the prologue of the trilogy as a whole.

Timaeus' Discourse

I. Prologue to the Discourse 27d5–29d6

After some further formalities, Timaeus begins the discourse proper by making some general introductory remarks about the status of the world of which he is going to give an account, and the status of his account of it. He begins with the broad metaphysical distinction between *what always is* (*to on aei*) and *what comes to be* (*to gignomenon*) *but never is*, a distinction familiar to readers of the *Republic*,[53] and the correlated epistemological distinction between understanding (*noēsis*), based on reason (*logos*), and opinion (*doxa*), based on sense perception (*aisthēsis*). Timaeus then argues that this world, being an object of sense

---

49. For discussion of these issues, see C. Gill [58].

50. For a recent account of the function of the Atlantis story in the *Timaeus* and *Critias*, see Pradeau [34].

51. In the *Timaeus* (27a–b), there is no hint that Hermocrates is to give a speech of his own, but he is placed in the lineup of speechgivers at *Critias* 108a–b.

52. Cornford ([14], p. 7) speculates that Hermocrates would have described "the re-emergence of culture in the Greece of prehistoric and historic times. . . . If so, the projected contents of the unwritten dialogue are to be found in the third and subsequent books of the *Laws*."

53. For example, see *Rep.* 518c, 534a.

perception, is a thing that has come to be, not one that always is. And since everything that comes to be requires a cause, the world must have a cause, that is, a maker. This maker, he assumes, will have looked at a model in fashioning the world[54]—a model which itself is either something that always is, or something that comes to be. Clearly, he argues, the model is of the former sort: this world is the most beautiful of things that come to be, and its maker the most excellent. The world, then, though a thing that has come to be, is nevertheless modeled after that which is intelligible and eternally stable.

Coupled to this description of the world's metaphysical and epistemological status is a description of the nature of the account Timaeus will go on to give of it. His general principle is that the accounts we give of things should share the fundamental characteristics of their subject matter: thus, accounts of what is unchanging and intelligible should themselves be stable and irrefutable. On the other hand, accounts of what is a "likeness" are themselves "likely" and therefore not subject to the same standards of rigor as the former accounts. Timaeus warns his audience not to expect accounts that are "completely and perfectly consistent and accurate" but only "accounts [that are] no less likely than any."

These introductory remarks invite closer inspection. In particular, we will want to know more about (1) the distinction between *what is* and *what comes to be* and the meaning of Timaeus' opening question; (2) what Plato means when he says that the world *has come to be*; and (3) what Plato understands by a "likely" account (*eikōs logos*) or story (*mythos*).

(1) *What always is* and *what comes to be but never is.*[55] It is customary in English to use the verb "to be" either synonymously with "to exist" (to say that something *is* is just to say that it exists) or as a link between a subject and a predicate ("John *is* a student"). Since the 1960s, however, studies of the Greek verb "to be" (*einai*) and its cognates have shown that this verb functions in a more complex way that does not easily map

---

54. As artist, the maker is an "imitator" (*mimētēs*, cf. *Rep.* X, 597e *ff.*) and so requires a model to imitate.

55. Some manuscripts include the adverb "always" with "what comes to be." See tr. p. 13 below, n. 13.

onto English usage.[56] In Greek as in English, the verb is used both by itself, without a grammatical complement, and with a grammatical complement. But even when it is used without a complement, it does not straightforwardly mean "to exist." To say in Greek that something *is* is to invite the question, "*What* is it?" (Compare: to say "A is eating" is to invite the question, "*What* is A eating?"[57]). It is now common among scholars to hold that in ancient Greek, for something to be is for it to be a subject for predication: to be *something*—a horse, say, or blue. This, however, is not to say that our concept of existence is absent from the Greek concept of being, or that it is always a mistake to translate *einai* as "to exist." It is only to say that "to exist" is not a distinct sense of a multivocal verb that can and should be isolated from its purported other senses.

To say, then, that something "always is" is not as such to say that it exists for all time but just as readily to say that it always is just *what* it is, something F or G. Hence it is easy to see how a thing's "always being" directly implies its changelessness. By the same token, to say that something "never is" is not as such to say that it never exists, but that it never is F, for any value of F—that it fails to possess any definite characteristic for any length of time. And if it is further described as something *coming to be*, then that thing is to be conceived as shifting constantly, moving, perhaps, *toward* being F or G but never completing the movement.

Nevertheless, even though in Greek "to be" does not as such mean "to exist" (and "to become" does not as such mean "to come into existence"), the question whether the world "has always been, having no origin (*archē*) of its coming to be or [whether it] has come to be, taking its start from some origin" (28b6–7) does seem to be the question of whether the world is something that has always existed or whether it had a beginning. Timaeus' answer that the world "has come to be" (*gegonen*—perfect tense) is the answer that the world is the sort of thing that has come into existence and thus did not always exist. He evidently does not (just) mean that it is the sort of thing that throughout its existence has always been in process. We should be careful, then, not to exclude existence

---

56. See Kahn [65] and [24], Brown [48].
57. See Brown [48], pp. 224–28.

from the semantic range of this verb in this opening section of the discourse.

How are we to interpret the "what?" question with which Timaeus begins (27d6–28a1)? That will depend on how we think Plato wants it to be answered. Perhaps Plato wants us to think back to the *Republic*, where the being/becoming distinction was used to refer to the contrast between Forms and sensibles. In that case, the answer to "What is *that which always is* and has no becoming?" is simply "Forms" or "a Form," and the answer to "What is *that which becomes* but never is?" is "sensibles" or "a sensible." In this case we have to supply the answer ourselves. But we can also read the question in such a way that Plato himself immediately answers it in the lines that follow. In that case, the question means something like, "What is characteristic of anything *that always is* and has no becoming—whatever it may be—and what is characteristic of anything *that becomes* but never is—whatever it may be?" Plato then gives the answer: the former is such that it is grasped by understanding, the latter such that it is grasped by opinion.[58] Read this way, the question invites us to think about what it is for anything to be without ever becoming, and what it is for anything to become without ever being. In favor of this way of reading the question is that it posits a conceptual connection between *being* and being grasped by understanding, and between *becoming* and being grasped by opinion based on sense perception. It is just such a conceptual connection that is needed for Timaeus' subsequent argument that the world, being visible, can only be grasped by opinion and is *therefore* something that *has come to be*, and *not* something that *always is* (28b7–c2).

(2) *The world "has come to be"* (gegonen). As we noted earlier (p. xxv), the straightforward assertion that the world "has come to be" presents a problem for those who take Plato's creation story metaphorically. Defenders of a literal interpretation point out that Plato's language is very clear. Timaeus asks whether the world has always been (existed) or whether it has come to be (28b4–7). This disjunction is surely intended as exclusive: if the world has indeed "come to be," then it is *not* the case that it has always been. Nevertheless, as we have seen, the metaphorical interpretation predominated among

---

58. See Zeyl [105], p. 122.

the later Platonists who distinguished various possible meanings of *gegonen* that did not require the world to have a temporal beginning,[59] and still finds defenders today. According to this reading, Plato means to stress not the temporal beginning of the world but its contingency, a feature of the world that does not preclude its everlastingness. It remains difficult, however, to reconcile such interpretations with Plato's straightforward language.

(3) *The nature of a "likely" account (eikōs logos) or story (mythos).* Not only in his prologue but frequently throughout the body of the discourse Timaeus reminds his audience that the account he gives is no more than "likely," warning them that they should not expect perfect consistency or accuracy.[60] We saw earlier that adherents of a metaphorical reading of the *Timaeus* find support in this qualification for their interpretation of the account. This, however, is implausible. The distinction between an account that is and one that is not "perfectly consistent and accurate" does not map easily onto the distinction between a literal and a metaphorical account. A metaphorical account is not as such a less consistent or accurate version of the corresponding literal one; and in any case the contrast Plato is drawing is not between literal and nonliteral accounts, but between apodeictic certainty and plausibility—a distinction that corresponds to the one between intelligible and empirical subject matters.

Probably what Plato means is that *within the constraints in which the story must be told* something like this account is the most plausible one can hope for. These constraints—metaphysical, epistemological, and aesthetic—make conflicting demands. The metaphysical constraint is that this world is caught up in unceasing becoming: its constituents are in flux, and any account of it cannot fail to reflect its elusiveness. The epistemological constraint is that this world is a sense object (or a collection of sense objects), and any account of it must reflect a grasp of it that is less than that absolutely firm grasp which we have of intelligible objects. On the other hand, the aesthetic constraint is that this world, being modeled after a perfect reality and fashioned by a most excellent maker, must

59. See n. 27 above.

60. See, for example, 30b7, 44d1, 48d2, 49b6, 53d5–6, 55d5, 56a1, 57d6, 59c6, 68d2, 72d7, 90e8. For other concessions, see 34c2–4.

resemble its model and its maker as much as possible in respect of beauty and goodness. The use of the word "likely" thus reflects both the limitations (it is no more than likely) and the validity (it is no less than likely) of the account.

II. The Discourse Proper 29d7–92c9

Why is there a world, and why does it have the features we observe it to have? To ask these questions is to ask for an explanation, or a set of explanations, of the existence and character of the world. The discourse of the *Timaeus* is fundamentally an explanatory account of the physical world.[61] It is not Plato's first attempt to provide explanations (*aitiai*)[62] of observable phenomena. In a famous passage of the *Phaedo* (95e–105c), Plato's Socrates laments the unavailability of the sort of explanations of things that would show why their existence and character is "for the best," explanations that we would call "teleological." He had hoped to find in Anaxagoras' theory of Intellect (*nous*) as the cause (*aitios*) of everything (97c2) just such an explanatory principle, but was disappointed to discover that the explanatory work in Anaxagoras' theory was done by the interactions of material principles. Rejecting explanations in terms of mechanical cause and effect and material conditions (such "explanations" merely state necessary conditions and as such are not explanations at all, 98c–99b), he settles instead for a "second voyage" (*deuteros plous*, 99c10–d1) that is, an account which, while not as adequate as the teleological account he would like to have, nevertheless has *some* explanatory capability. This is the account in terms of things' participation in Forms: the answer as to why a thing is (or becomes) F is just that it participates (or comes to participate) in the Form of F (the "safe," "simpleminded," or "ignorant" *aitia*) or that it comes to participate in G, given that (in certain relevant cases) the Forms of G and F are so related that, necessarily, if anything is G, then it is F (the "subtle" *aitia*). It is clear, though, that despite these formal explanatory accounts, as we may call them, Socrates' preference remains for a teleological account (99c6–9), and we may suppose that Plato continued to believe

---

61. This point is well argued, among others, by Strange [93].

62. An *aition* (pl. *aitia*) is a factor that is (causally) responsible for the existence of an object or a state of affairs. An *aitia* (pl. *aitiai*) may also be such a factor or may be an explanation, that is, an answer given in response to the question, "Why does *x* exist?" "Why is *x* F?" Compare Vlastos [97], 78–81, and M. Frede [57], 128–30.

that observable phenomena are not adequately explained and hence understood unless in terms of their place in an economy designed "for the best."

In the *Timaeus* Plato offers just such an account of the world. The world is the product of Intellect (Anaxagoras' *nous*), personified in the figure of a divine craftsman (demiurge). The overarching goal of Intellect is to fashion a world that is as good and as beautiful as the character of the materials out of which it is made will allow. These materials, too, he now concedes, figure in an explanatory account of the world, not indeed as "primary" but as "auxiliary causes" (*sunaitiai*, 46c–e). Their inherent properties impose constraints on what may or may not be made out of them, and to a considerable extent dictate the properties, and hence the behavior, of the objects fashioned out of them. These constraints collectively represent the causal role of Necessity, and limit what the craftsman, who is not omnipotent, can make of these materials and the extent to which he can make them good. Nevertheless, in his wisdom the craftsman is for the most part able to turn these constraints to good advantage, to serve in the production of things that are good and beautiful (this is the "persuasion" of Necessity by Intellect—48a2–5), although there will be occasions in which Intellect must make concessions to Necessity.[63]

The explanatory roles that are assigned to Intellect and Necessity provide a tripartite framework for the composition of the discourse as a whole, a structure that Plato very deliberately follows. Its first major section (29d7–47e2) describes "what has been crafted by Intellect" (47e4). In this section Timaeus explains the creation of the world, its character as a supremely rational animal, and its uniqueness in terms of the underlying requirements of goodness and beauty. The composition of the world's body as well as that of its soul follows mathematical principles of harmony and proportion. The "heavenly race of gods," the fixed stars, the sun, moon, and planets are created to serve as markers of time, and the fixed stars are spread throughout the heavens as an adornment, their unceasing and unvarying rotations and revolutions displaying their perfection. Other orders of living beings, in particular human beings—soul and body—are also created to manifest, to the extent their material constitution allows, that same intelligence, beauty, and goodness that belong to the world as a whole.

---

63. Most famously, at 74e–75d. See below, p. lxxxi.

The second major section (47e–68d) discusses "the things that have come about by Necessity" (47e5). Here the focus is not on the purposive arrangement of parts, but rather on the nature and properties of the basic material constituents of those parts. These basic constituents—fire, air, water, and earth—have traditionally been called "elements," but Plato rejects the designation. These stuffs are themselves aggregates of geometric solid particles whose surfaces are composed of tiny triangles. But their articulated construction as geometric solid particles is the work of the divine craftsman: prior to his intervention there were only "traces" of fire and the others, fleeting and coincidental configurations that only approximated their subsequent natures, randomly churning about in "the wetnurse of becoming" (52d4–5), the "Receptacle" that both moves them and is moved by them. (A complex metaphysical argument, intended to show both the need for and the nature of the Receptacle, prefaces this section.) It is the erratic movement of the Receptacle that causes and preserves a state of nonuniformity and hence of constant motion and, as a consequence, causes the primitive corpuscles, the geometrical solid particles, to break up into their constituent triangles, and those triangles to be reconfigured into new particles, thus bringing about intertransformations among three of the four elemental bodies that are constituted by similarly shaped triangles (fire, air, and water). The mechanics of the collisions, breakups, and reconstitutions are determined strictly by the motions of the Receptacle and the various geometrical properties of the particles and, ultimately, of the triangles, and not by any overriding controls exercised by the craftsman. As such, they represent the causal influence of Necessity; the craftsman may indeed make beneficial use of them ("persuading" Necessity), but he is unable to eliminate or overrule them. The generation and behavior of varieties of fire, air, water, and earth, as well as combinations of these, are similarly explained by the interactions of their primitive particles as determined by Necessity. And, finally, as these corpuscles interact with the sense organs of percipient subjects, "disturbances" of the appropriate kinds are received by the soul, and the objects perceived come to have the various perceptual properties these subjects perceive them as having. A theory of perceptual experience, together with the experiences of pleasure and pain, completes this section of the discourse.

The final section of the discourse (69a6–92c) is set to "weave together" (69a8) the explanatory roles of Intellect and Necessity in an account that begins with the psychophysical formation of man: the immortal soul previously created (41d–42d) is encased in the head, but because the conditions of embodiment require sense perception, a mortal soul is required as well. This soul is subdivided into two parts, each situated within the trunk of the body but separated by the midriff: the superior part above it, in the heart, and the inferior part below it, in the belly.[64] The physical organs and other body parts all have a supporting role in maximizing intelligent and virtuous life, and to the extent that their material constitutions render them suitable for that task, we see how Necessity is for the most part made subservient to Intellect.

The origin of physical diseases is attributed to "unnatural occurrences and changes" (82a7–8) in the body's elemental constituents, in some cases consisting of the reversal of those processes by which the bodily parts were originally constituted. The more intense diseases of the soul are brought on by excessive pleasures and pains, and these, too, have a physiological basis. Both kinds of diseases are remedied by proportion, achieved and maintained by a regimen of exercise for the soul and the body— Intellect thus once again prevailing over Necessity. By studying the harmonies and revolutions of the world, human beings restore the native revolutions of their souls and achieve that excellent life intended for them by the gods. The discourse concludes with an account of the generation of women, the physiology of human reproduction, and the generation of birds, land animals, and fish.

A. The Craftsmanship of Intellect: 29d7–47e2

(i) The World Is an Intelligent, Living Thing (29d7–30c1)

Having established that the world, as something that has come to be, has a cause (a maker), Timaeus now proceeds to explain why the maker made a world: the maker was good, and any good being wants anything else to be as good as it can be. This argument might seem incomplete. As it stands, it explains why the maker would make a *good* world, but not why he should make a world at all. Why should it be good that a world exists rather than not? We should remember, however, that Plato's worldmaker does not create *ex nihilo*. The antecedent situation prior to his creative activity is not nothing, but the independent existence of a primordial chaos (30a2–6). What requires explanation is thus not why

---

64. See 69c–70a.

anything (besides the worldmaker and his intelligible model) exists at all, but why the primordial chaos should not be left as it is. And for this the explanation given is perfectly adequate: "Order [is] in every way better than disorder."

Does this requirement of maximal excellence mean that for Plato, as later for Leibniz, this world is the "best possible" world? Yes and no. This world, constrained as it is by Necessity, is surely not the best *logically possible* world. Whether or not such a world can exist, or whether an omnipotent deity can create such a world, is not an issue that bears on the *Timaeus*. On the other hand, the requirement does imply that this world is the best one there can be, given the ineradicable limitations imposed by Necessity.

The requirement of maximal excellence also explains why the world should be a supremely rational animal: an intelligent being is more excellent than one lacking intelligence, but intelligence cannot come to exist in anything apart from soul (i.e., in anything that is not alive). It is sometimes objected that the latter premise requires the creative Intellect (represented mythically by the divine craftsman) also to be "ensouled," yet soul is something that is said to be created by the craftsman (34b–36d). The creative Intellect, then, is an unexplained and anomalous exception to the premise. The objection misses its point, however: the premise says only that nothing can (come to) *have* intelligence apart from soul, and this does not rule out the possibility of the existence of something that *is* intelligence (or Intellect), quite apart from soul.[65]

(ii) The World Is Unique (30c2–31b3)

As an image of a model, the world—an intelligent, living thing—is modeled after the eternal Living Thing. What is this? Clearly it is a Form, or a unified constellation of Forms, including all the varieties of Living Things that are to be reproduced in the created world. Its excellence requires that it be complete—that no species of Living Things be left out; similarly, the excellence of its image requires that all these varieties be instantiated in our world.[66]

---

65. So argued by Hackforth [64], p. 445; Robinson [37], p. 102, n. 25. In any case, the generalization expressed in the premise seems to apply only to things that come to be.

66. Does the eternal Living Thing comprise all the Forms there are? One reason for thinking that it does: any instantiation in the created world of any Form is a copy of some aspect of the eternal model. Since no model other than the eternal Living Thing is mentioned in the *Timaeus*—and assuming that there are no unin-

How many images of this model are there? Only one, Plato argues. Its model is one, and could not be more than one. Making this world "like the complete Living Thing in respect of its uniqueness," the worldmaker made no more than one world.

In proposing this argument for the uniqueness of our world, Plato has been accused by some of making a fundamental category mistake.[67] Suppose we distinguish between the property or complex of properties of a Form that make it that particular Form—the Form of F as opposed to G—and the properties every Form has that distinguish it qua Form from sensibles—eternity, changelessness, and so on, and call the former the *proper* attribute(s) of a particular Form, and the latter its *formal* attributes. Any craftsman making a copy of a particular Form, so the objection goes, will copy only its proper attributes; its formal attributes are impossible to copy. Since the uniqueness of the Form of Living Thing is one of its formal properties (each Form qua Form is one), only a "mad craftsman" would attempt to copy its uniqueness. Critics of this objection respond, however, by pointing out that Plato does not just invoke the uniqueness of the Form of Living Thing as a formal property of that Form; rather, he *argues* for its uniqueness, as follows: since (1) the Form of Living Thing is complete (i.e., inclusive of all the various intelligible Living Things there are) and (2) if there were, say, two Forms of Living Thing, neither would be complete (because each would fail to include the other), thus (3) both would be parts of some third Form of Living Thing which includes them both, the last alone being complete. According to this way of reading Plato's argument, the completeness of the Form of Living Thing is one of its proper attributes, and its uniqueness is inferred from its completeness. The same argument applies mutatis mutandis to the created living thing: if it is to be complete, it cannot fail to be unique.[68]

---

stantiated Forms—all Forms that are instantiated are presumably included in that model. On the other hand, the eternal Living Thing may be intended as a model just insofar as it is to account for the nature of the created world as itself a living thing, and for the variety of kinds of living things in that world; in that case the craftsman (1) looks to the Living Thing only for those aspects of the created world that make it and many of its contents living things, and (2) looks to other Forms for models for the remaining aspects of that world.

67. Keyt [66].

68. This line of argument is presented (with minor variations) by Parry [82] and [83] and by Patterson [84].

(iii) The World's Body (31b4–34b9)

It is not a fundamental assumption of Plato's cosmology that if there is to be a world, it must be physical. Rather, he derives the world's corporeality from its status as a becoming thing. From its corporeality he then derives its visibility and its tangibility, and from these in turn its composition of fire and earth. He then proceeds to argue for the necessity of air and water: they are intermediaries, required for the bonding of fire and earth. The whole chain of reasoning is explanatory: we observe a world whose ultimate constituents are (or appear to be)[69] the four traditional elements, and we ask for an explanation of their existence. The explanation is serial, and overtly teleological: each of the elements is set in an explanatory context that culminates in the world's metaphysical status as a thing that comes to be.

The world, however, is not just an aggregate of elements—it is a unity, and its unity must also be explained. The unity of the world is not simply an observed datum: it follows from the requirement of what is best (*kalliston*, 31c2). And this unity is expressed in geometrical proportion (*analogia*, c3): since proportion is the best possible (because most unified) arrangement of diverse constituents, and since this world is the best world that could be made, this world's constituents are arranged proportionately.

According to a much discussed sentence (31c4–32a1),[70] geometrical proportions are applicable to numbers, to "powers" (properties that vary in degrees of intensity, e.g., the powers of heat and cold, 33a; cf. also 56c3–4) and to "bulks" (masses that vary in size or weight). Since the world's body is a three-dimensional object (*stereoeide*, 32b1), it is a "bulk," and thus qualifies for a proportionate quantitative distribution of elements, a distribution that requires not one but two middle terms. The end terms of the elements making up this bulk are fire and earth, the middle terms air and water. Thus, "what fire is to air, air is to water, and what air is to water, water is to earth" (32b5–7). Plato does not say what the actual proportions are—evidently no specific proportions are entailed by the requirement of what is best.[71]

---

69. For the qualification, see below, pp. liv–lv and lxvi.

70. For the interpretation of this sentence followed here and in the translation, see Pritchard [88].

71. Could the proportionate distribution be *qualitative* as well (or instead)? If we think of the elements in terms of the traditional "opposites" (as Aristotle does in

The completeness and uniqueness of the world, already established earlier (Section ii above) are guaranteed further by the
exhaustive consumption of the four constituents, which also en-
sures it against aging and disease. The shape of the world is
spherical, the most uniform of shapes, and its external surface
smooth. It requires no sense organs or limbs since it has no external environment, and is thus self-sufficient. It is set to move in
perpetual rotation, a motion that Plato associates in particular
with understanding and intelligence.[72]

(iv) The Composition of the World's Soul (34b10–36d7)

After discussing the construction of the world's body, Timaeus
proceeds with an account of the origin of the world's soul. He
emphatically points out that in presenting the latter account subsequently to the former he is not implying that the body has priority
over the soul; quite to the contrary, the rule of soul over body
requires both its greater excellence and seniority.

The construction of the world soul takes place in four stages:
(1) the creation of the three preliminary mixtures of divisible/
indivisible Being, Sameness, and Difference, and from these the
creation of the final mixture; (2) the partitioning of the final mixture into two series; (3) the "filling of the intervals"; and (4) the
creation of the circles of the Same and the Different. The details
of these stages are discussed in the note to the translation (p. 20,
n. 25). Here we might ask why Timaeus has the soul acquire this
particular constitution.

The soul's construction out of a mixture of intermediate Being,
Sameness, and Difference, themselves ingredients produced by
mixing indivisible with divisible Being, Sameness, and Difference,
is required by the cognitive capacities the soul is to have, in
particular by the kinds of judgments it is supposed to be able to
make. Subsequent passages make it clear that these are judgments
of sameness and difference,[73] that is, judgments about "things
that are" to the effect that they are the same as, or different

---

his own theory of material elements) of hot versus cold and wet versus dry, with
fire (hot/dry) and earth (cold/dry) being the extreme opposites, their opposition
might be mediated by air (hot/wet) and water (cold/wet) and the proportionality
might be expressed as follows: hot/dry (fire) :: hot/wet (air) :: cold/wet (water) ::
cold/dry (earth). In this case we would have a proportion of "powers."

72. For an account of Plato's association of rotation with intelligence, see Lee [70].

73. 37a2–b3, also 43e8–44a4 and 44b4–7.

from, other things. Relying on the well-known ancient principle of cognition that "like is known by like," Plato requires that these basic ontological relations be themselves manifested in the soul.[74]

In a difficult passage (37a2–c5), Timaeus explains how this is supposed to work. After the division of the mixture and the filling of the intervals (stages 2 and 3: 35b1–36b5), the now harmonically proportioned soul-stuff is formed into two bands, the circles of the Same and of the Different, the plane of the latter positioned at an inclined angle to that of the former and set to move in a contrary direction.[75] Because the soul is in part composed of a mixture of indivisible being and divisible being, it will recognize anything it "comes in contact with" (37a6) as a thing that is either a Form (indivisible being) or a particular (divisible being).[76] It will then judge whether that thing is the same as or different from something else and the various respects in which it is the same or different or both.[77] When the "thing that is" is a Form, the judgments the soul makes about it constitute knowledge; when it is a particular, the soul's judgments constitute opinion.[78]

---

74. Compare 37a2–b3. Thus when the object of the soul's cognition is a Form (indivisible Being), the soul is able to grasp that Form's "sameness" in virtue of its own indivisible Sameness, and that Form's "difference" in virtue of its own indivisible Difference. Similarly, when the object is a particular (divisible Being), the soul can grasp its sameness in virtue of its own divisible Sameness within it, and its difference in virtue of its divisible Difference.

75. This division into two bands is the basis for the later introduction of the two heavenly circles or bands of the daily revolution of the stars, and that of the sun annually along the ecliptic.

76. We might wonder whether Plato's designation of perceptible particulars as belonging to "divisible being" is consistent with his denial, at 28a2–3 and later at 38a8–b5, of being to things that come to be. Plato is quite ready to admit that things that come to be are among the things that there are (cf. also 52d3); here "being" is not a status word, but simply indicative of the thing's actual existence, whatever its status.

77. It is natural to see in this passage a rudimentary theory of predication according to which any judgment of the form, "X is Y" is a judgment that X is the same as Y, and any judgment of the form "X is not Y" is a judgment that X is different from Y. If so, the passage has implicit connections with Plato's explicit discussions of positive and negative predication in the *Sophist*. The *Sophist*, however, emphatically rejects the idea that all statements of the form "X is Y" are identity statements, and appears to distinguish between judgments of identity and predication (Frede [20], Owen [79]), thus moving well beyond the rudimentary theory of the *Timaeus*.

78. Plato assigns judgments of sameness and difference about indivisible Being (Forms) to the rotational activity of the circle of the Same, and judgments of sameness and difference about divisible Being (particulars) to the contrary and

(v) The Creation of Time and the Celestial Clock
(37c6–39e2)

We have seen that the model after which the world was made is eternal. Plato's account of the model's eternity follows from his determination to exclude all becoming from that which truly is, and so the eternity in question cannot be temporal everlastingness, duration without beginning or end, but must be timeless eternity (37e4–38a6).[79] The image of this model is excluded by its status from qualifying for such timelessness: as a becoming thing it can be "eternal" only in a derivative sense, and so it is set in unceasing, regular and uniform motion. This motion produces time, described as "an . . . image . . . of eternity, moving according to number" (37d6–7; cf. 38a7–8).[80]

The "movement" of time "according to number" indicates both the everlasting flow of time and its divisibility into parts that are numerically discrete. Each (sidereal) day-and-night, (lunar) month, and (solar) year is distinguished from others by the fact that each completes a single cycle in the course of which the heavenly body that is the "marker" for that time period returns to its original position (39c1–5). These parts of time are not necessarily proportionate to each other: for example, the lunar month is incommensurable with the solar year, and is just in excess of 29½ days.

"Time, then, came to be together with the heavens . . ." (38b6).

---

inclined rotation of the circle of the Different. Although no reason for this is spelled out, we may infer that it is the uniformity (and hence indivisibility) of the motion of the circle of the Same, and the multiformity (divisibility) of the circle of the Different that makes each the appropriate agent for its assignment.

79. For an account of Plato's concept of timeless eternity and his debt to Parmenides, see Owen [80].

80. It is possible, though difficult, to construe the Greek at 37d5–7 differently as follows: "at the same time as he brought order [to the universe], he would make the heavens, an eternal image moving according to number, of eternity remaining in unity. This [number], of course, is what we now call time." On this reading it is the heavens, not time, that is the image of eternity; time is the "number" according to which the heavens move. It is difficult, however, to square this reading with 38a7–8, which explicitly refers to *time* (and not the heavens as such) as that which "imitates eternity and circles according to number." I have therefore retained the (traditional) translation and take Plato's point as follows: by setting the heaven in motion the Craftsman creates time, a supervenient aspect of that motion. Just as the heaven itself (and indeed the whole visible universe) is modeled after the eternal Living Thing, so its temporality is modeled after the Living Thing's eternity.

The difficulties that attend the notion of the "coming to be" of time are well known. Things that come to be, come to be "in" time. If time itself came to be, what did it come to be "in"? A higher-order time? And if time came to be, when did it come to be? How old is time? Was there anything "before" the coming to be of time? These questions are particularly acute for Plato, for he is prepared to speak about "being, space, and becoming, three distinct things that existed even *before* [my emphasis] the heavens came to be" (52d3–4). If we follow the literal reading of the creation story, we will have to conclude that time and the world have a literal beginning, and that a certain state of affairs actually did precede the coming to be of time. As we have seen (p. xxiv), defenders of the literal reading distinguish between time as a measurable flow, indexed to the periodic motions of the heavenly bodies, and unmeasured flow, which yet entails irreversible temporal succession, such that if A occurs before B, anything in A's past cannot be in B's future.[81]

The claim is often made that for the Greeks, time was cyclical.[82] What could this mean? And does the *Timaeus* support such an account? The claim cannot mean, without absurdity, that identical times "come around" periodically in a never-ending sequence: in that case each complete revolution of time would be indistinguishable temporally from its predecessor and its successor. At best the claim can mean that the same events always recur at any given point in the revolution. Now whether or not other Greeks (the Stoics, for example) might have thought this to be the case, there is no reason to think that Plato is among them. For one thing, although time is *measured by* the various circular movements of the various heavenly bodies, and indeed cannot be measured apart from those movements, there is no need to suppose that for Plato *time itself* is in periodic motion: this is to confuse the supervenient character of temporality with the sidereal and planetary movements it is supervenient upon.[83] And even though time is divisible into discrete units (day-and-night, month, year) by

---

81. See n. 40 above. For a response to the possible objection that "was" and "will be" are "forms of time that have come to be" (37e4) and hence that there could be no past and future in any precosmic "time," see Mohr [28], pp. 64–66.

82. For example, by Cornford [14], p. 103.

83. The "*circling* [of time] according to number" (38a7–8) is derivative of the circular motion of the heavenly bodies; temporal progression (cf. time's "*moving* according to number" [my emphasis], 37d6–7) could just as well be conceived as linear. See Vlastos [96], p. 409.

virtue of these movements, which endlessly repeat themselves, it hardly follows that the series of events that takes place in time is endlessly repeated.

(vi) Celestial Circles and Planetary Motions: Some Interpretive Issues

We saw earlier (p. xxxvii) that the demand for the world's excellence requires that it be rational and thus that it should have a soul (30b), and have just seen how the soul's cognitive activity dictates its composition. But cognitive activity is not the only function of soul in the cosmology. The soul is also to be the mover of the world's body, or, more specifically, of the bodies of which the world's body is composed. These are (1) the realm of the fixed stars; (2) the sun, moon, and the five planets[84]; and (3) the earth and all the living things on or near its surface. The earth, itself a sphere, is at the center of the cosmic sphere, and the fixed stars are at its circumference. The fixed stars are moved around the center of this sphere exclusively by the rotational movement of the circle of the Same, causing them to revolve in an unvarying pattern around the world's center, though each star also rotates around its own center (40a7–b2). The motions of the planets are much more complex, and what Plato has to say about them is often unclear and controversial.

Plato ascribes the motion of the sun, moon, and planets to the movement of the circle of the Different. This circle is subdivided (we are not told how) into seven smaller, unequal, and concentric[85] circles, each of which provides the trajectory and movement of one of the "wandering stars." The original undivided circle of the Different was described as rotating within the circle of the Same, in a direction contrary to the latter's rotation, and its plane (the ecliptic—the mathematical line on the celestial sphere that marks the annual path of the sun around the earth) at an angle[86] to the plane (the sidereal equator) of the circle of the Same.[87] The planes of the seven smaller circles are not necessarily parallel to

---

84. The seven "wandering" stars—the moon, the sun, and the five planets known to the ancients: Mercury, Venus, Mars, Jupiter, and Saturn.

85. Concentric also with the center of the circle of the Same, that is, the center of the universe.

86. Of 23.5°.

87. See the translation, pp. 21–22, and tr. n. 26.

the ecliptic[88] or to each other, but vary within the outer limits of the Zodiac, that broad band of familiar constellations of fixed stars which is bisected by the ecliptic. The planets, then, are subject both to the east-to-west movement of the circle of the Same, as are the fixed stars, and to the contrary movement of the Different over which the motion of the Same prevails.[89] It is this subjection to two contrary cosmic movements—movements, furthermore, that intersect each other at a considerable angle—that results in the appearance of irregularity of the planets' orbits.[90]

Several details of the account have given rise to considerable discussion and debate, as follows.

(1) *The movements of the seven planetary circles.*

    36d4–7: "He set the circles to go in contrary directions: three to go at the same speed, and the other four to go at speeds different from both each other's and that of the other three. Their movements, however, were all proportionate to each other."

Here "the circles" evidently refer to the seven unequal circles produced by the division of the circle of the Different, and a natural reading of the passage suggests that some of these circles go in a contrary direction from others, that is, that if some go from west to east, say, others go from east to west. But if these circles are divisions of the previously undivided circle of the Different, and that circle *as a whole* moves from west to east (see tr. n. 26), what could possibly explain the contrary movement (from east to west?) of some of its parts?

To this difficulty some have responded by assigning to at least some of the circles a third motion in addition to that of the Same and of the Different, which impels some of them to move faster than the movement of the Different, though in the same direction,

---

88. If they were, there would be no need to divide the circle of the Different: the sun, moon, and planets could each be placed on an undivided circle at various distances from Earth. The sun's path, however, is in the plane of the ecliptic.

89. 36c7–d1, 39a1–2. This explains why the rate of a single revolution of the fixed stars, once every 24 hours, is much faster than even the fastest revolution (at angular velocity) of the "wanderers," that of the moon, once every 28 days. The rates of revolution of the sun, Mercury, and Venus are on average equal: once every 365 days, or a solar year; those of Mars, Jupiter, and Saturn are resp. once 1 year plus 322 days, once 11 years plus 315 days, and once 29 years plus 166 days (see Vlastos [41], p. 33).

90. For a vigorous defense of the view that the movements of the planets are not irregular but only appear so, see Vlastos [41], pp. 99–100 and 101–2.

and others in a contrary direction and thus slower than it. Cornford, a proponent of this solution, attributes this "third force which modifies the motion of some of the planets" to the voluntary motions that these heavenly bodies can exert independently in virtue of having souls, that is, principles of self-motion.[91]

Critics of this view point out that there is no textual basis whatever for postulating a "third force" involved in planetary motion, and that the self-motion assigned to the planets in virtue of having souls is, like that of the stars, that of axial rotation exclusively.[92] A better alternative, consistent with the Greek though not necessarily the most natural reading of it, is to construe the text as saying that *each* of the seven circles is moving in two contrary directions at the same time, that is, both in the east-to-west direction of the circle of the Same and the west-to-east direction of that of the Different.[93] If read in this way, the passage anticipates the point at 39a5–b1.

(2) *The "contrary power" of Mercury and Venus.*

> 38d2–4: The Dawnbearer [the Morning Star, or Venus] and the star said to be sacred to Hermes [Mercury] he set to run in circles that equal the Sun's in speed, though they received the power contrary to its power. As a result, the Sun, the star of Hermes, and the Dawnbearer alike overtake and are overtaken by one another.

What is the "power contrary [to the sun]" that Mercury and

---

91. See Cornford [14], pp. 82–87, who invites us to imagine something like a circular moving walkway (as perhaps in a large modern airport), rotating at a constant speed. Three passengers (representing the sun, Mercury, and Venus) stand still at various points on this walkway as it moves. One (representing the moon) runs fast *ahead* in the same direction as the movement of the walkway, so that it overtakes each of the stationary passengers approximately thirteen times in the course of a single rotation of the walkway. Three other passengers (representing Mars, Jupiter, and Saturn) walk *in the reverse direction* from the movement of the walkway, at different speeds, though presumably in no case quite so fast as to equal the motion of the walkway.

92. See Dick [17], pp. 125–26, and Vlastos [41], pp. 109–10.

93. So Vlastos, following Cardini. See Vlastos [41], p. 108. Another solution, suggested by Dicks [17], pp. 128–29, as "possible (though perhaps unlikely)" is to take the "circles" that are set to go in contrary directions to refer not to the seven circles created by the division of the circle of the Different, but to the circles of the Same and the Different. If this is correct, then Plato is saying nothing controversial; he is simply repeating his point made just moments earlier. This solution is well criticized by Vlastos, ibid.

Venus receive?[94] Cornford, the proponent of the "third force" account of the contrary motion of the seven circles, suggests that this power, called on as it is to explain why Mercury and Venus "overtake and are overtaken by" each other, is the nonuniformity in the speed of each of those two planets, a factor he ascribes (not surprisingly) to the self-motions possessed by each of the planets as ensouled beings. The contrary power is thus identical with that which accounts for the contrary directions of the seven circles at 36d4–7.[95] Critics of this position point out, however, that this again requires the idea of a "third force," which has already been shown to be suspect. Since the "contrary power" is invoked to explain the observation that Mercury and Venus "overtake and are overtaken by" each other, Cornford's account is inconsistent with his own earlier account of the contrary motions of the planetary circles (above, p. xlvi).[96]

Perhaps the best way to explain what Plato means by the contrary power is to ask what account he might have given of the observable phenomenon of the sun, Mercury, and Venus overtaking and being overtaken by one another. The answer to that is not far to seek. Later, at 40c, Timaeus speaks of the "dancing movements" of the celestial gods, "their juxtapositions *and back-circlings (epanakuklēseis,* c5)." These "back-circlings" refer to the phenomenon of retrogradation, in which a planet appears to come to a stop in its eastward motion, move temporarily in a westward direction relative to the fixed stars, stop, and then resume its eastward motion. Plato's use of the term *epanakuklēseis* indicates that he was familiar with this phenomenon. Another way to describe the same phenomenon, which can also be observed in the motions of Venus and Mercury relative to one another and to the sun, is to ascribe the "power of contrary (movement)" to the bodies in question.[97]

---

94. The literature on this issue is extensive; see Vlastos [41], p. 107.

95. Since, on Cornford's view, the contrary directions of the planetary circles also include the directions of the outer planetary circles (of Mars, Jupiter, and Saturn), he extends the "contrary power" of the present passage also to those planets. See Cornford [14], p. 109. Dicks [17], p. 126, objects.

96. Dicks [17], p. 126, points out that Cornford's account of the "contrary power" conflicts with his "moving walkway" analogy (above, n. 91), which requires not only that the sun, Mercury, and Venus travel at the same speed in the same direction, but also that they are stationary relative to each other. See Dicks also for other criticism of Cornford, [17] pp. 126–27.

97. So Vlastos [41], pp. 107–8.

(3) *Was Plato familiar with Eudoxus' theory of homocentric spheres?*
     39c5–d2: "As for the periods of the other bodies [the five plan-
             ets], all but a scattered few have failed to take any
             note of them. Nobody has given them names or in-
             vestigated their numerical measurements relative to
             each other. And so people are all but ignorant of the
             fact that time really is the wanderings of these bodies,
             bewilderingly numerous as they are and astonish-
             ingly variegated."

Just before this passage, Timaeus has defined each of the various units of measured time—(sidereal) day/night, (lunar) month,
and (solar) year—in terms of a single revolution of the outer
heavens, the moon, and the sun, respectively. In the passage, he
explains why there are no recognized units of time associated
with the revolutions of the five planets. His explanation seems
to have three parts: (1) the revolutions of the five planets have
been studied only by "a scattered few"; (2) no "names" have been
assigned to the temporal durations of a single revolution of each
of the planets (corresponding to "day," "month," and "year" in
the cases of the stars, the moon, and the sun); and (3) no study
has been made of the numerical proportions among the temporal
lengths of their revolutions, because of the vast complexity of
their movements. Even so, Timaeus insists, such proportions—
known or not—do exist. These revolutions are not of indefinite
or undefinable duration, and they, too, no less than the revolutions
of the stars, moon, and sun whose regularity *is* capable of explanation, constitute time.

The issue raised by the passage is this: According to an ancient
testimony, Plato had posed the following challenge to the astrono-
mers of his day: "What uniform and orderly motions must be
hypothesized to save the phenomenal motions of the stars?"[98] We
are told that Eudoxus, a younger contemporary of Plato's and an
associate in the Academy, was the first to answer the challenge
by proposing his famous theory of homocentric spheres.[99] It has
been argued that Plato was probably familiar with this theory
when he recorded his astronomical observations in the *Laws*,[100]

---

98. The challenge and Eudoxus' response to it are reported by Sosigenes, a second-
century C.E. astronomer, as cited in Simplicius' commentary on Aristotle's *On the
Heavens* 488.18–24. For discussion, see Vlastos [41], pp. 110–11.

99. For a lucid account of Eudoxus' astronomy, see Dicks [17], pp. 151–89.

100. See *Laws* 822a4–8, where the view that the moon, sun, and five planets
"wander" is rejected.

but not yet when he wrote the *Timaeus*, where, as we see here, the "wanderings" of the five planets are described as "bewilderingly numerous" and "astonishingly variegated."[101] It is not clear, however, whether we can infer from the *Timaeus*, or even from the *Laws*, either that Plato was or that he was not familiar with Eudoxus' theory at the time of writing either of these dialogues. Even though the *Timaeus* uses, and the *Laws* forbids the use of, the predicate "wandering" in reference to the planets, both dialogues agree that the orbits of the planets are in fact determinate and regular, even though in the *Timaeus* at least Plato is in no position to propose a theory by which their regularity can be understood. It could well be that at the time Plato was writing the *Timaeus*, Eudoxus (perhaps one of the "scattered few") was still working out his answer to Plato's challenge and that by the time Plato wrote the astronomical passage of the *Laws*, he had completed it.

(4) *Does the earth rotate on its axis?*

> *40b8–c3:* "Earth he devised to be our nurturer, and, because it is packed around [or: winds around] the axis that stretches throughout the universe, also to be the maker and guardian of day and night. Of the gods that have come to be within the heavens, Earth ranks as the foremost, the one with greatest seniority."

Scholars are divided over the question as to whether this passage, especially if its correct reading is "winds around" (*illomenēn*, as opposed to *eillomenēn*, "packed around") implies the axial rotation of the earth. The main arguments on this issue are as follows.

(a) Plato emphasizes that the movement of the world soul, and thus also of the circle of the Same, pervades the entire universe, from the center on out to its periphery (36e2–5). Since the center of the universe is the center of the earth, the earth, too, from its center on out, rotates (relative to "absolute space") with the circle of the Same, on the polar axis. However, if this were the only movement the earth is subject to, the revolution of the fixed stars would be unobservable, since the earth would be following along with the movement of the Same, thus keeping the same fixed stars overhead at each place on its outer surface. Since we do manifestly observe the revolution of the fixed stars, the earth must also rotate *relative to the Same*.

---

101. This argument is made by Owen [81], pp. 325–26, as part of his more elaborate argument for an earlier dating of the *Timaeus*. See above, "The Place of the *Timaeus* in the Order of Plato's Dialogues," pp. xvi–xx.

It is the latter rotation that would presumably be referred to
by the expression "winds around the axis." What, then, explains *this* rotation? There are two possibilities: (1) Just as
each of the stars and planets, being a divine, intelligent ensouled being, is assigned rotational movement (40a7–b1), so
Earth, the "foremost" of the created gods, rotates along the
polar axis of the universe in a direction exactly contrary to
the movement of the Same and at an angular velocity exactly
contrary to that of the Same. The effect is that the second
rotation cancels out the first, so that relative to "absolute
space" Earth does not rotate.[102] Alternatively (2), the center of
Earth is also the center of the circle of the Different, so that
like the sun, moon, and planets, Earth is also subject to its
motion. The axial rotation that is supposed to explain that the
circle of the Same actually does move relative to the position
of Earth is simply the rotation effected by the motion of the Different.

Both alternatives have problems. Against the first is the
fact that it overlooks the motion of the Different, also centered
in Earth's center and thus subjecting Earth to its contrary
movement. Against the second is the fact that Earth's alleged
rotation is described as being "around the axis that stretches
throughout the universe," and this seems to be the axis of the
circle of the Same, perpendicular to the sidereal equator, and
cannot be the axis of that of the Different.

(b) The reading *illomenēn* is not as well attested as, and should
be rejected in favor of, *eillomenēn*.[103] On this view there is no
reference to axial rotation in the passage at all. Earth, rather
than spinning in a direction contrary and equal to the movement of the Same, is able by virtue of its divine status—
supreme among the created gods—to resist the force of the
movement of the Same (and presumably that of the Different
as well) and stay still relative to absolute space.

(vii) The Creation of Living Things (39e3–47e2)

The next phase of the creative process is the population of the
world with the four kinds of living things (i.e., animals) that are
represented in the eternal model. These, Timaeus says, are (1)

---

102. This interpretation is defended by Cornford [14], pp. 120–34.
103. See Dicks [17], pp. 132–33 and p. 239, n. 181.

"the heavenly race of gods," both the celestial bodies and the gods of popular religion; (2) winged and airborne creatures; (3) creatures that live in the water; and (4) creatures that have feet and dwell on land.[104] In the descriptions that immediately follow, he confines himself to the creation of the gods and of human beings, leaving until the end of the discourse the accounts of the airborne and aquatic creatures and of nonhuman land dwellers (91d6–92c3).

The fixed stars and the planets, including the sun and moon, have already been introduced as markers of time[105]; now they, together with Earth, are introduced as celestial divinities, visible counterparts of divine Living Beings within the composite Living Being that serves as the world's model. The fixed stars are made out of fire and are given a spherical body. They are set to rotate upon their axes, so that they "would always think the same thoughts about the same things" (40a8–b1)[106] and to revolve with the circle of the Same.[107] Earth, we have seen, is best interpreted as standing still about the center of the universe.

Timaeus concludes the astronomical part of his discourse by referring once again to the complexities of the celestial dance. There is no doubt, however, that no matter how complex in description or even physical demonstration,[108] Plato's belief in the regularity and synchronicity of the movements of the heavenly gods remains firm.

The origin of the popular divinities receives short shrift by Timaeus. Such an account is "beyond our task," and "we should follow custom" in accepting traditional accounts. Plato has very little to say in general about popular religion that reveals either an endorsement or a repudiation of popular theology. What is clear from the paucity of references in the dialogues is that

---

104. Each kind thus inhabits one of the four elemental regions of the universe.

105. It is a common mistake to restrict the role of time marker to the planets (e.g., Cornford [14], p. 117). The fixed stars, and not any of the planets, mark off by their complete revolution one complete day-and-night.

106. See n. 72 above.

107. The sun, moon, and five planets (but not Earth) are also made primarily of fire, and (unlike Earth) also rotate upon their axes (as Earth does not). The paths of their revolutions are not, of course, solely determined by the movement of the Same.

108. Plato may be suggesting that the use of a sufficiently complex physical model might successfully demonstrate these various celestial phenomena.

theorizing about the status of the popular gods falls outside the
scope of Plato's philosophical, even religious, interests.

The immortality of the created gods is not guaranteed by their
own constitutions: what has been created is in principle capable
of perishing. It is, however, guaranteed by "a greater, more sovereign bond"—the will of the divine craftsman.[109]

The task of creating the three remaining kinds of living things
is now put into the hands of the first kind, the created gods, to
ensure their inferiority to those gods (41c2–3). The account here
and in the last main section of the Discourse focuses exclusively
on the creation of male human beings. The creation of women
and nonhuman animals is a consequence of the possibility of
human moral and intellectual failure.[110]

The (initially human) souls are mixed of the same ingredients—although of inferior grade—as the soul of the world (35a1
ff.), to give them the same cognitive capacities (cf. 43e8–44b7 with
37a2–c5). Their number equals that of the stars (each of which,
of course, has its own soul, already created by the craftsman
when he created the stars); and each soul has its home star as its
"carriage," by which it is transported through the outer regions
of the universe.[111] Having viewed "the nature of the universe"
from that perspective, all these souls are "sown into" Earth and
the planets.[112] It is disputed whether this "sowing" is the actual
populating of Earth *and* the planets by human and (subsequently)
other living beings, or a stage in the migration of these souls from
their stars into the planets, to await their incarnation exclusively
on Earth.[113]

Once incarnated "of necessity,"[114] the living organisms—un-

---

109. The sovereignty of the craftsman's will is nevertheless limited by Necessity.
See below, p. lxxix.

110. See pp. lxxxviii–lxxxix below.

111. The image is strongly reminiscent of the description of the procession of
souls at *Phaedrus* 247a *ff.*

112. The home stars of these souls are subject exclusively to the revolution of the
Same. Once the souls are "sown into" the planets, they become subject to the
contrary revolution of the Different as well. Their salvation (rewarded by their
return to their native stars) will consist in subjecting their physical bodies to the
rule of "the revolution of the Same and uniform" that persists within them.

113. The former alternative is favored by Taylor [39], pp. 258–59, and rejected
by Cornford [14], p. 146, in favor of the latter.

114. Whereas the "sowing" of the souls into the planets is clearly an activity of
the craftsman (and hence of Intellect), their actual incarnation seems to be a
consequence of Necessity. The task subsequently given to the created gods of

like the world as a whole—require the capacity of sense perception, since they—unlike it—will live in an environment that presents them with "forceful disturbances." This capacity is taken to include the capacity to experience pleasure and pain, as well as love (*erōs*), fear (*phobos*), and spiritedness (*thumos*) and their opposites, strong emotions aroused by the disturbances communicated to their souls via sense perception.[115] The salvation of the incarnated souls will depend on the degree to which they can master these emotions: their lives will be just and good, and thus exempt from further reincarnations to live happily on their home stars to the extent that they succeed in this. To the extent that they fail, they are destined for a succession of reincarnations that will end only when these emotions are mastered by reason. The success or the failure of the souls will be their own responsibility: neither the craftsman nor the created gods bear any blame.

These lesser gods proceed to fashion the human body[116] from the four elements and to "invest" it with the soul. As a material object the body is subject to the erratic shaking motions of the Receptacle (52d4–53a7; cf. 57d3–58a2), partly neutralized but far from eliminated by the craftsman. The uncontrolled movements of a newborn infant reflect this agitation. The newly incarnated soul is also buffeted from the outside by the "nourishment-bearing billow" and by the disturbances produced in it as the sense organs are impacted by other material objects. The cumulative effect is that the motions of the Same and the Different within the soul are "mutilated and disfigured," rendering the soul incapable of exercising its cognitive function, which, like that of the world's soul, is to make appropriate judgments of "sameness" and "difference." Only in the course of time and with the proper nurture and education will the soul's orbits reestablish themselves, enabling it to judge correctly.

Timaeus concludes the section that I have called "the craftsmanship of Intellect" with some remarks about the construction of the human head and body and the mechanics of vision, including

---

fashioning the human body (42e6–43a6) thus seems to be a concession to Necessity unworthy of the creative powers of the craftsman himself.

115. The psycho-physiology of sense perception will be discussed in more detail at 61c–68d, esp. 64a–65b. See below, pp. lxxiv–lxxvi. Sense perception, along with pleasure and pain and the strong emotions, is assigned to the "mortal" type of soul, constructed by the lesser gods (69c6–d6) "as was necessary" (d5).

116. The construction of the human body will be described in detail in the third section of the discourse, at 69a *ff.*, after the articulated construction of each of the elemental bodies has been explained in the second section.

an explanation of mirror imaging. Elaboration must await later discussion (beginning at 69c5), since such physiological subject matter concerns "auxiliary causes" and as such properly belongs to the later sections of the discourse. His present purpose is to explain the teleology of these mechanics: the body exists to serve the head, and the head, including its power of sight, exists to serve the soul (46e7–47c4): Sight communicates to the soul the periods of the revolutions of the heavenly bodies, giving us "number and . . . the idea of time," making possible astronomical inquiry and eventually philosophy. As we observe and come to understand the "orbits of intelligence in the heavens," we are in a position to "apply them to the revolutions of our own understanding" and thereby "stabilize the straying revolutions within ourselves."[117]

B. The Effects of Necessity: 47e3–69a5

As we have seen, the account offered so far of the creation of the world and the living things (animals) within it has been primarily teleological. Timaeus now turns to an account of what we might think of as the physics of the world, the basic natures and properties of the four primary bodies—fire, air, water, and earth—out of which the body of the world has been constructed (31b4–32c4). Are these four kinds the ultimate material constituents of the world?

In the physical theories of Plato's predecessors, the ultimate *archai*, or primary principles of the physical world, were three-dimensional bodies of some sort, whether of a single kind (monism) or of irreducibly diverse kinds (pluralism). For example, Empedocles had held that there were four primary bodies (which he called "the four roots of all things"), earth, water, air, and fire. By mixing with and separating from one another, these four bodies alternately came and ceased to constitute the mid-sized objects of our experience. Plato follows Empedocles in speaking of these as the four primary "kinds" or "bodies." He does not dispute the existence of these four primary bodies. But he parts company with Empedocles in two very significant ways. First, he denies that these four bodies have the status of ultimate constituents. As he puts it, far from being "elements" (*stoicheia*, lit. "letters"), they do not even have the status of "syllables," that is,

---

117. See below, pp. lxxvii–lxxviii.

penultimately basic entities (48b6–c2). His reasons for the denial and the insistence will become clear at 52d4 *ff.* As we shall see there, in his account these four bodies are themselves composites, artfully constructed by the craftsman out of elementary triangles, assembled so as to form three-dimensional "particles" of various sorts. It is these triangles, and not the bodies constructed out of them, that he takes to be the true ultimate constituents of the world. Second, Plato's predecessors had no metaphysics to undergird their physics. Empedocles, for example, had no answer to the question of why anything that is fire has *that* particular nature, rather than some other. Plato, on the other hand, insists that there be an answer, and he famously answers it in terms of his theory of Forms: whatever is fire has the nature it has because it participates in, or resembles, the Form of Fire.

It is a cardinal doctrine of Plato's metaphysics that nothing in the world of sense experience retains its character permanently, and from this it follows that even the traditional "elements" are impermanent: what is water now will at some later time no longer be water. This metaphysical requirement is corroborated by sense experience: we actually see how these elemental bodies are transformed into one another.[118] But if there is something that can be water at one time and not at another, what is that "something" in its own right?

It is this worry that leads Plato to postulate the mysterious "third kind" of entity, in addition to the two previously postulated kinds. These were (1) the changeless and intelligible model of the world: the Forms (particularly the constellation of Forms that makes up the Eternal Living Thing), and (2) the visible, coming-to-be "imitation" of that model: the world and its components, fashioned by the craftsman after the likeness of that model.[119] But the character of this third kind is "difficult and vague" to describe (Timaeus says that it serves as a "receptacle" or "wetnurse, as it were" of all becoming, 49a5–6), and anyhow some explanation is needed of why it must be introduced at all.

In the difficult passage that follows, Timaeus provides an

---

118. As it turns out, only three of the four (fire, air, and water) are transformable into each other. The exception of earth is explained at 54b5–d2. See also Section (iv), "The Construction of the Four Primary Bodies," below, pp. lxvi–lxix.

119. This description of the "imitation" may appear to beg some questions that will be raised later. Up to this point in the discourse, however, only the world and its contents have been described in terms of an "imitation" of a model.

argument for the necessity and the nature of this Receptacle. Since both the correct translation of Plato's Greek in the passage and the metaphysical theory that is supposed to emerge from it have been debated during the last fifty years, the passage deserves separate discussion.

(i) A Much-Disputed Passage: The Receptacle (49a6–50a4)

The translation of the passage given in this book (pp. 38–39) is an example of what I shall call the "traditional" translation ("*T*"). I set this translation side by side against another translation of the same lines, preferred by many scholars, which I shall call the "alternative" translation ("*A*"). For ease of comparison, I give a version of *A* that departs from the version of *T* given in the text only in those respects that are vital to the differences in grammatical construction and consequent interpretation. The differences between the translations are italicized.[120]

Traditional Translation ("T")	*Alternative Translation ("A")*
Now then, since none of these appears ever to remain the same, which one of them can one categorically assert, without embarrassment, *to be some particular thing, this one,* and not something else? One can't. Rather, the safest course by far is to propose that we speak about these things in the following way: what we invariably observe becoming different at different times—fire, for example—to characterize *that, i.e., fire, not as "this," but each time as "what is such,"* and	Now then, since none of these appears ever to remain the same, *concerning* which one of them can one categorically assert, without embarrassment, *that this is some particular thing,* and not something else? One can't. Rather, the safest course by far is to propose that we speak about these things in the following way: what we invariably observe becoming different at different times— fire, for example—to characterize *not this, but what on each occasion is such,* as "*fire*," and

---

120. Prior to 1954 the traditional translation was all but universally adopted, without recognition that the text might also be read in the alternative way. The original version of *A* (from which other versions depart in matters of detail) was proposed and defended by Cherniss [50]. An analytical version of *A* is offered by Lee [72], p. 5. Other versions of *A* are given in Mills [74], pp. 154–56 and Mohr [75], p. 141. Support for *A* (though not a version of the translation) is found in Silverman [92]. Versions of *T* with criticisms of *A* are offered in Gulley [62], pp. 53–54, Zeyl [106], 129–30, and M. L. Gill [60], 34–35.

speak of water not as "this," but always as "what is such." And never to speak of anything else as "this," as though it has some stability, of all the things at which we point and use the expressions "that" and "this" and so think we are designating something. For it gets away without abiding the charge of "that" and "this," or any other expression that indicts them of being stable. It is in fact safest not to refer to it by any of these expressions. Rather, "what is such"—coming around like what it was, again and again—that's the thing to call it in each and every case. So fire—and generally everything that has becoming—it is safest to call "what is altogether such." But that in which they each appear to keep coming to be and from which they subsequently perish, that's the only thing to refer to by means of the expressions "that" and "this." A thing that is some "such" or other, however—hot or white, say, or any one of the opposites, and all things constituted by these—should be called none of these things [i.e., "this" or "that"].

to call not this, but what is ever such, "water." And never to call it by any other term—as though it has some stability—of all the terms we use which we think have a specific meaning when we point and use the expressions "that" and "this." For it gets away, without abiding the charge of "that" and "this," or any expression that indicts them of being stable. It is in fact safest not to call them (i.e., the fire and water we see) these several things (i.e., "fire," "water," etc.). Rather, what—coming around like what it was again and again, in each and every case—is such, is the thing to call that way (sc. "fire" or "water"). So what is altogether such it is safest to call "fire," and so with everything that has becoming. But that in which they each appear to keep coming to be and from which they subsequently cease to be, that's the only thing to refer to by means of the expressions "that" and "this." But what is some such or other, however—hot or white, say, or any of the opposites, and all things constituted by these—[it is safest] not to call it (sc. the Receptacle) any of these.

It will be helpful to highlight the precise ways in which these translations differ, before commenting on the significance of these differences for an overall interpretation of 48e–52d.

The differences between the two translations can be focused on their different renderings of the following schema (following the word order of the Greek):

"... not *this* but *what is such* to call *fire (water)*. ..." ("*mē* touto *alla*
to toiouton *prosagoreuein* pur [hydōr]," 49d5–7)

T-readers take this schema as: "not to call fire 'this' but rather
'what is such,' that is, not to refer to the fire or water that we see
("phenomenal" fire or water) as "this" but rather as "what is
such." *A*-readers take it as: "not to call this, but rather what is
such 'fire,' " that is, not to apply the term "fire" to *this* (i.e., some
particular bit of phenomenal fire or water we might point to),
but rather to things that are *such* (on these, more below). The
Greek can be read either way. So what is the material difference
between *T* and *A*?

According to *T*, Plato is telling us to speak of phenomenal
fire, water, and so on, as things that are "such," not as things that
are "this." He is not telling us not to call them by their usual names
("fire," "water," etc.),[121] but to understand their status differently.

What is it, on this reading, for bits of phenomenal fire and so
on to be "suches" and not "thisses"? Although not all *T*-readers
would agree, many would say that in this context, Plato's view
is that for something to be a "this," it must be self-subsistent, that
is, be whatever it is in its own right rather than by virtue of
something else. The Forms are self-subsistent, and, Plato will
claim, the Receptacle is as well (50b7–8), and hence each of them
is properly a "this" (49e7–50a2). By contrast, instances of phenomenal fire and so on lack self-subsistence: the fact that they seem
to be intertransformable (49b7–c7) suggests that none of them is
what it is in its own right: if one and the same thing can be now
fire and later air, then it cannot be either fire or air in its own
right; at best its being fire is a temporary characteristic of it (as
its being yellow, or bright, would be). What we ordinarily call
fire is, qua fire, merely a "such."

By contrast, according to *A*, Plato is telling us that given these
apparent constant intertransformations, it is not correct to refer
to instances of phenomenal fire and so on by their usual names.
Since any bit of phenomenal fire does not remain fire, we should
not call it "fire" at all, not even when it momentarily appears as
fire. To use a term such as "fire" to refer to something is to imply

---

121. At 69b6–7 Plato says that in the precosmic chaos the element traces (on
which see below, p. lxvii) did not qualify for the "names we now use to name
them." The implication seems to be that the artfully constructed elemental bodies
of the ordered world do qualify.

that the referent has a stable character, which neither this fire nor that fire (any instance of fire to which we might point) can claim to have. Only things that "are always such," that is, things that have the character always, and not just for a fleeting moment, are the proper referents for terms like "fire."

What sorts of entities are the "such"-things, on this interpretation? Not all *A*-readers agree. An obvious candidate is a Form, for example, the Form of Fire. It is, after all, a standard Platonic doctrine that Forms are the primary referents of our terms, at least for those terms for which there are corresponding Forms, since Forms display (or better: are) the stable natures designated by the meanings of those terms. While some proponents of the alternative translation have opted for this identification,[122] most have not: after all, the Form of Fire *is itself* what (the nature of) fire is, and not (merely) *such as* or *like* fire (to say that something is *toiouton* is to say that it is *like* something, not that it *is* that thing). Moreover, the "such"-things are described as entering and leaving the Receptacle (49e7–50a1), whereas Forms are explicitly said not to enter "into anything else anywhere" (52a3). The entities in question must then be distinct from Forms: in fact, most proponents of the alternative translation identify them as "perpetually identical characteristics" or "distinct and self-identical characteristics,"[123] or "recurrent, stable and determinate characters."[124]

(ii) "Images," Particulars, and the Receptacle (48e2–53b5)

There are some significant interpretive issues at stake in this dispute. The issues revolve primarily around the following three interconnected questions, which I will discuss separately: (1) What justification is there for identifying the "images" or "copies" (in the translation, "imitations"—*mimēmata*) of a Form either as phenomenal particulars (as in *T*) or as self-identical or recurrent characteristics (as in *A*)? (2) What different accounts of phenomenal particulars do the two readings require, and how can these accounts be supported from the text? (3) What different accounts of the nature and function of the Receptacle are implied by each of the readings?

---

122. For example, Mills [74].
123. Cherniss [50], pp. 124, 128.
124. Lee [72], p. 27.

(1) *The Form "copies."* Both *T*- and *A*-readers agree that the "imitations" of the Forms, whatever they are, are the "such"-things
of the text. As we have seen, though, *T*-readers take these to
be phenomenal particulars, correctly understood. *A*-readers,
on the other hand, identify them as the self-identical or recurrent characteristics, the "such"-things of the alternative translation. Several *T*-readers have asked whether there is any
justification for introducing what appears to be a further ontological realm, distinct both from Forms and from particulars,
into the metaphysical scheme. They object that Plato clearly
speaks of *three* ontological "kinds": (a) Forms, (b) sensible
particulars, and (c) the Receptacle (48e5–49a6, reprised at
50c7–d4, 51e6–52b2). Would not these recurrent characteristics constitute a *fourth* kind and thus disrupt the scheme?[125]
A-readers have responded by challenging the view that the
items in (2) are the sensible particulars as ordinarily understood. They are either the self-identical characteristics (Cherniss [50], Silverman [92]), or particular instances of those characteristics reflected in the Receptacle (Lee 1966).[126] *T*-readers,
however, find this unsatisfactory. If the realm of these items
is supposed to be already familiar to us from the metaphysical
scheme of the first part of the *Timaeus* now under revision,[127]
it surely can be none other than the realm of "that which
comes to be" of 27d6–28a4: the visible, created world and
its contents.

(2) *The nature of phenomenal particulars.* *T*-readers take Plato not
to be changing what counts as a particular—particulars are
the familiar entities they have been all along—but to be providing a new metaphysical analysis of their nature and status:
they are not, as we formerly might have thought and as up
to this point in the discourse Timaeus might seem to have
been treating them, self-subsistent entities (as, for example,
Aristotle thinks of primary substances in the *Categories*), but
are (parts of) the Receptacle (51b4–6), the latter being modified

---

125. The objection is hinted at by Gulley ([62], p. 64) and pressed by Zeyl ([106],
pp. 134–35). Neither Cherniss nor Lee appears to have considered the objection;
in fact, Lee ([73], p. 367) has Plato distinguishing *"four* items" (his italics), none
of which is identifiable with sensible particulars as such, in the course of 48e–52d.

126. Mills answers the objection by arguing that the "such"-things are to be
identified with the Forms. For criticism, see Zeyl [106], pp. 134–35.

127. See n. 119 and text above.

by the imprints it takes on so as to present them as appearances (50c2 *ff.*). Since the Receptacle takes on a rapid succession of imprints (cf. the "gold example" at 50a4–b5), a particular will change rapidly over time without, however, necessarily ceasing to be that same particular. Its identity over time is preserved by virtue of the fact that it remains the same part of the Receptacle,[128] its neutral, self-subsistent *substratum*. *A*-readers, on the other hand, argue that particulars are not "things" at all: like reflections produced in mirrors,[129] they are the products of the exits and entrances of the "such"-things (as *A* understands these) into the Receptacle. The temporary sojourns of the "such"-things project apparent properties onto or into the Receptacle, and these apparent properties are just what the particulars are.[130] Again, such an analysis (and analogy) has not recommended itself to *T*-readers. It requires, in their view, an unnecessary and in any case too radical departure from whatever it is that Plato has been referring to by "things that become and pass away" in the previous part of the dialogue.

(3) *The Receptacle.* The account that Plato gives of the Receptacle itself is at best obscure (as he admits, 49a3–4) and at worst incoherent. Here are some descriptions of it:

(a) it is that "in which" the "such"-things (on either interpretation) make their appearance, and "from which" they perish (49e7–50a1);

(b) it receives all things without departing from its own character in any way and without ever taking on the characters of the things that enter it; it is modified and reshaped by those things, which make it appear different at different times (50b7–c4; cf. the preceding "gold analogy" at 50a4–b5);

(c) it is totally devoid of any characteristics of its own (50d5–51a3);

(d) it is "space" (*chōra*) which provides a "fixed site" (*hedra*, lit. "seat") for all things that come to be (52a8–b1);

(e) it is shaken by, and in turn shakes, the things that

---

128. For discussion of what it means to be a "part" of the Receptacle, see below, p. lxiii.

129. See, for example, Lee's distinction between "substantial" and "insubstantial" images and his use of the mirror analogy (Lee [73], pp. 352–57).

130. For a well-developed account of what a particular is on the *A* translation, see Silverman [92], pp. 87–95.

enter and leave it, and its agitation produces a separation of the "four kinds" into stratified regions (52d4–53a7).

The two predominant ways of thinking about the Receptacle which emerge from these descriptions is that the Receptacle is, first, a neutral "stuff" in which various characteristics temporarily inhere, but, second, also a space or place in which things appear and from which they disappear. Descriptions (b) and (c) encourage the former conception, while (a) and (d) appear to support the latter. Description (e) suggests the latter, insofar as the things that shake and are shaken by the Receptacle are to be thought of as its contents, but the former as well, to the extent that it itself, and not just its contents, both causes and undergoes motion. Can the "stuff" and "space" conceptions of the Receptacle be reconciled?

Viewed as "stuff," the Receptacle seems to anticipate the idea of "prime matter," traditionally associated with Aristotle.[131] The Receptacle thus serves as the material substratum or subject of change. The particulars of sense experience are then similar to compounds of "form" and "matter." They are composed (1) of the various bits of Receptacle stuff they're made up of (their "matter"), and (2) of the characteristics (their "forms") these various Receptacle bits continually come and cease to exhibit by virtue of their participation in various Forms. On the other hand, if the Receptacle is viewed as "space," it is essentially a container or medium through which the "such"-things (on either account) travel.

It is not difficult to see that *T*-readers, who favor the "substratum" view of the Receptacle, tend to think of it as a neutral stuff, which is temporarily characterized in its various parts by an array of properties these parts possess by virtue of their participation in Forms. They claim support from the gold example at 50a4–b5: just as the gold is the "stuff" constantly being reshaped, now as triangle, now as something else, so the Receptacle is the stuff that is constantly being reshaped, now as fire, now as water, and so on. *A*-readers, on the other hand, prefer to think of the Receptacle as a medium, or space, in which those properties intermittently occur as a result of the stable Forms' being reflected in this

---

131. It is, however, sharply disputed whether the idea of "prime matter," a completely neutral and characterless stuff, can properly be attributed to Aristotle.

medium. They favor the analogy (not used by Plato in the passage) of a mirror: just as a mirror reflects the objects in front of it, producing an image that has no independent reality whatever, so the Receptacle reflects the Forms, which produce in it images that have no independent reality, either.

It might seem at first that these two ways of representing the Receptacle are irreconcilable and that therefore Plato's account is incoherent. Consider, for example, what it would mean to be a "part" of the Receptacle. (Any "part" [*meros*] of it that gets ignited from time to time, says Timaeus, appears as fire, and so on [51b4–6].) If the Receptacle is space, its parts would have to be identified by spatial coordinates, and would thus be logically incapable of traveling through space. Anything moving through the Receptacle from one place to another could then not be identified as the same part of it throughout. This would be troublesome for the *T*-reading, which favors viewing the parts of the Receptacle as the substrata of phenomenal particulars. On the *T*-reading, what secures the identity of particulars traveling through space is identity of substratum traveling through space; thus the same part of the Receptacle must be capable of traveling through space. On the other hand, if the Receptacle is stuff, it then becomes a mystery why it should be called space.

A solution to these issues might lie in reexamining the notion of *chōra*, regularly translated as "space." Our contemporary notions of space can mislead us here. We tend to think of space in terms of Newtonian or Eisteinian physics, but that is hardly what Plato had in mind. Plato's notion of *chōra* is better captured by our concept of "room" as in "room to move around in." It is a theory-independent truism that anything which moves requires room in which to move. And there is no reason why something cannot be both stuff and also the room in which that stuff moves. Think of an agitating container holding a liquid. As the liquid sloshes around, currents may begin to form within it—that is, some "parts" of it will travel through other "parts" of it. The parts through which the currents travel is the room. But any part of the room may become a traveler as well. Thought of in this way, the Receptacle is a plenum or stuff, then, not sheer (empty) space, which nevertheless also provides the room for certain parts of itself to travel through. And if this picture is somewhere near correct, the dual roles assigned to the Receptacle are not at odds with each other. (I leave the reader to ponder how this picture of the Receptacle comports with each of the *T*- or *A*-readings.)[132]

(iii) The Argument for Forms (51b6–52d4)

In middle dialogues like the *Phaedo* and *Republic*, Plato presents and develops his theory of Forms as the foundation of his metaphysical, epistemological, and ethical theories. It is striking, however, that in these dialogues any argument in support of that theory is entirely absent.[133] The present passage in the *Timaeus* appears to be the only one in the Platonic corpus which purports to be an argument for the existence of Forms. As it is, it is self-consciously compressed.[134] The distinction between Forms and sensibles, Plato maintains, is entailed by a distinction between understanding (*nous*) and true opinion (*doxa alēthēs*).[135] Given this entailment, that is the distinction Timaeus wants to argue for in the present context.

Understanding and true opinion, Timaeus says, are such that (1) we can come to have one without the other, and (2) the one is not like the other. He glosses (1) by stating that we come to have understanding by instruction and true opinion by persuasion. The distinction is reminiscent of one drawn in the *Gorgias* (454c–e):

---

132. Another virtue of this picture is that it helps to integrate the description of the Receptacle in (e) with the earlier descriptions. It helps to distinguish the Receptacle from its contents, and allows both for its ability to shake and be shaken by these contents, while the latter are nevertheless parts of it, and it is the medium through which they move and without which they could not exist.

133. When the Forms are introduced in the *Phaedo*, at 65d4, it is on the basis of agreement that "we say" they exist. Even the famous argument at 74a9–c6 is not an argument for their existence (again, "we say" [74a9–10] that they exist) but for their ontological distinctness from sensibles. The theory is said to have the status of a hypothesis at 100b5–6. And the argument with the sightlover in the *Republic* (477a ff.), far from arguing for Forms, does not even mention them as such. The argument's conclusion is that the sightlover fails to have knowledge of sensible "beautifuls," not that there is a Form of Beautiful.

134. ". . . neither must we append a further lengthy digression to a discourse already quite long . . ." (51c7–d1).

135. For this entailment we are no doubt to be reminded of the argument at *Republic* 477c ff. according to which the distinctness of knowledge (*epistēmē*) and opinion (*doxa*) as powers or capacities (*dunameis*) entails that they both accomplish different things and are set over different objects. The *Republic* argument assumes what the *Timaeus* argument seeks to establish: that these two are in fact different powers.

there Socrates distinguishes between two types of persuasion, one that produces knowledge and one that produces (true or false) conviction (*pistis*) without knowledge. The former is "the persuasion that comes from instruction" (*peithō didaskalikē*) and the latter "the persuasion that comes from being convinced" (*peithō pisteutikē*, 455a1). Clearly the "persuasion" of the *Timaeus* passage corresponds to the latter of the two types of persuasion in the *Gorgias*, and the "instruction" to the former. Timaeus glosses (2) by stating that understanding always involves a true account, while true belief lacks any account. Both (1) and (2) are tied together in that Plato is apt to define instruction as a rational process, in which the learner is rendered able to "give an account" of the subject matter being learned, and (conviction-producing) persuasion as an irrational one that leaves the persuaded party firmly convinced yet unable to give any such account. He further notes that understanding and true opinion differ in that the former "remains unmoved by persuasion" while the latter "gives in" to it.

Having established to his satisfaction that Forms do exist, Timaeus turns next to discussing the epistemic status of each of the items in his now tripartite ontology: Forms, images, and the Receptacle. The Forms, as we already know, are the insensible objects of understanding; the things that come to be are the perceptible objects of opinion; and the Receptacle ("*chōra*" here), which, like the Forms, "exists always and cannot be destroyed" (52a8–b1), "is apprehended by a kind of bastard reasoning. . . ." (b2). What this "bastard reasoning" is like we are not told. Perhaps what is meant is that our grasp of the Receptacle can be arrived at only by way of a difficult and obscure process of reasoning like the one Timaeus himself employed in the foregoing part of the discourse. Unlike sensible images, the Receptacle is not perceptible, and unlike Forms, it has no intelligible nature of its own. Not only must its existence be inferred, but its role can be illustrated only by cumbersome analogies themselves drawn from sense experience.

Timaeus concludes this section with what might be considered yet another "bastard" argument for the necessity of the Receptacle: given that there are images of Forms (which *ex hypothesi* are not Forms themselves and so do not "have as their own" what Forms have as their own), their characteristics in virtue of which they are images of Forms must inhere in something that exists to support their role as images. So the image must be "in" something, as, for example, an image of Abraham Lincoln must be

"in" marble or bronze or oil on canvas or glossy paper, in order
to be an image.[136] There must, then, be a Receptacle for any image
of Forms to be *in*.

(iv) The Construction of the Four Primary Bodies
(53a2–55c6)

Having concluded his extended metaphysical argument for the
necessity of the Receptacle, Timaeus returns to the issue he had
in hand that led him to that argument: the nature and properties
of the four primary bodies, fire, water, air, and earth. He is now
in a position to explain these basic natures and properties. We
saw earlier that Timaeus explicitly denies that these four "kinds"
themselves have the status of "elements," that is, the irreducibly
basic constituents out of which everything else is constructed but
which are not themselves constructed out of anything else more
basic (above, pp. liv–lv). They are constructed by the craftsman
out of what are presumed to be the truly ultimate constituents,[137]
the two forms of right-angled triangle, the half-equilateral isosceles and the scalene.

Timaeus argues to the existence of these two ultimate constituents as follows (53c4–d7): (1) Each of the four kinds is a "body."
(2) All bodies have "depth," that is, are three-dimensional. (3) All
things having depth are comprehended within surfaces. (4) All
surfaces bounded by straight lines are composed of triangles.
(5) All triangles are composed of right-angled triangles, either
isosceles or scalene. The conclusion that he takes to follow from
these premises is thus (6) that each of the four kinds is composed
of either isosceles or scalene right-angled triangles.

The argument raises several questions not addressed in the
discourse. First, why the switch from "surfaces" in (3) to "surfaces
bounded by straight lines" in (4)? Why are curved lines, and thus
surfaces that are spheres or parts of spheres, ruled out? Second,
isn't the isosceles right-angled triangle itself divisible into two
scalene right-angled triangles and therefore not really basic?[138]
Third, isn't *every* right-angled triangle of either sort, like all triangles, divisible into further right-angled triangles as (5) postulates,

---

136. See Cherniss [52] for discussion of this passage.

137. He is careful, however, not to insist dogmatically that these triangles are the
ultimates (53d4–7).

138. Of course the two resulting scalene right-angled triangles do not have the proportions of the "selected" ones (immediately below)—they are not half-equilaterals.

thus rendering each of the elemental right-angled triangles infinitely complex? If these elementary triangles are the "atoms" of Plato's physics, what renders them immune from further (and regressively infinite) divisibility? It is not clear how Plato might have answered these questions.

Before describing the construction of each of the four kinds out of the elementary triangles, Timaeus recapitulates (cf. 30a) the precosmic scenario: in the maelstrom produced by the agitation of the Receptacle and its contents, "traces" of each of the four kinds would appear in different regions of it, each of which would tend to move to its own region by the action of the Receptacle, which is compared to that of a winnowing sieve (52e6–7). What are these "traces"? Presumably they are collections of corpuscles consisting of various accidental combinations of irregularly shaped surfaces, combinations that fall far short of the artfully constructed polyhedra to be described later but coincidentally resembling them in some ways and, to that extent, behaving like them in tending to appear in different regions of the Receptacle.[139]

The craftsman begins his work by selecting a particular version of the scalene right-angled triangle: the half-equilateral, proportioned this way: $1 : \sqrt{3} : 2$. It is chosen because it is the most excellent (a claim that Timaeus declines to defend). Triangles of these proportions are needed because only they can constitute, in an array of configurations, the equilateral triangles of various sizes that are to become the faces of three of the five regular polyhedra, the tetrahedron, the octahedron, and the icosahedron, respectively the basic corpuscles of fire, air, and water (see Figure 1). These equilateral triangular faces, then, are the "syllables" constructed out of the "letters" of the half-equilaterals. As for the isosceles right-angled triangle, no particular version of it need

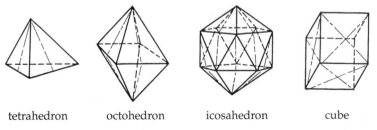

| tetrahedron | octohedron | icosahedron | cube |

Figure 1

---

139. For a different view, see Cornford [14], 199–202.

or even can be chosen, since all such triangles have identical proportions: $1 : 1 : \sqrt{2}$. These triangles will constitute, also in an array of configurations, squares of various sizes.[140]

What explanatory job is the analysis of the four primary bodies into triangles of just these proportions supposed to do? Plato wants to account for two kinds of processes, both of which he discusses at some length. The first is the intertransformation of three of the four primary bodies. The second is the appearance of distinct varieties within each primary body.

To begin with the first. Each face of each of the polyhedra that constitute the basic corpuscles of fire, air, and water is an equilateral triangle. The tetrahedron has four, the octahedron eight, and the icosahedron has twenty such faces. So far forth, then, these faces might be interchangeable, leading to the emergence of any one or more of the three out of any one or more of the others. But there is a complicating factor: each of the four kinds is distributed over many different varieties, so that when intertransformations occur, it is not just from one kind to another, but from a particular variety of one kind to a particular variety of the same kind or of another. This leads directly into the second point: how are we to distinguish among the varieties of any particular kind? The answer is that each kind is "graded" into varieties, and the only criterion by which they may be graded is quantitative: a corpuscle of one variety of air, say, can differ from a corpuscle of another variety only by being a bigger or smaller octahedron. If, then, each of the equilateral faces of each of these polyhedra must be able to come in different sizes, it can only be because it is composed of a greater or lesser number of elementary half-equilaterals (assuming the latter to be of some fixed minimal size throughout). These are the different "arrays of configuration" of primary half-equilaterals noted earlier, and illustrated in Figure 2.[141] Similarly, smaller or bigger squares can be constructed out of elementary isosceles right-angled triangles of a given size, to serve as faces of differently sized cubes, corpuscles of different varieties of earth.

---

140. If we are to assume that all the primitive half-equilaterals are all of the same (minimal?) size, and similarly the primitive isosceles right-angled triangles, then different arrays of configurations are needed to constitute equilateral triangles and squares of different sizes.

141. It is something of a mystery why Timaeus posits (at 54d7–e3) as the standard composition of the equilateral triangle the one that is composed of six elementary

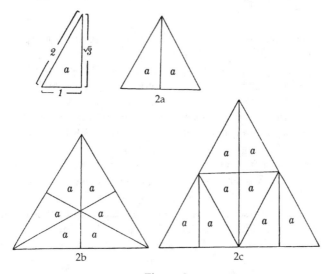

Figure 2

Why does Timaeus exclude earth from this intertransformation among the kinds? He can hardly have empirical grounds for doing so. He acknowledges that the dissolution of earth into the other kinds or its emergence from them is on a par with the intertransformations of the other three as far as appearance goes (54b6–8).[142] No doubt Plato could, if pressed, explain the appearance away.[143] The exclusion is driven by his theoretical commitments. Plato's contemporary Theaetetus had constructed the five regular solids, which included the cube as well as the three polyhedra already assigned. That Plato was eager to assign a distinct solid to each of the four kinds is confirmed by his desire to find a cosmological role for the fifth regular solid, the dodecahedron, which, because it most nearly resembles a sphere, is "assigned" to the world as a whole (55c4–6).

---

half-equilaterals (Fig. 2b), not the one composed of two (Fig. 2a). For an educated guess, see Cornford [14], p. 234.

142. Apparently at least two of Plato's predecessors accepted the appearance at face value. See Xenophanes (DK 21 A33[5]) and Heraclitus (DK 22 B31). Aristotle criticizes Plato for the exclusion of earth (on the ground that this is at variance with what we observe) at *De Caelo* 360a1–7.

143. As is done on his behalf by Vlastos [41], pp. 81–84.

(v) The Interactions among the Four Primary Bodies
    (55d7–58c4)

Having constructed the corpuscles of each of the four primary
bodies in this way, Timaeus now proceeds to give an account of
the physics of their intertransformations. The mechanisms by
which these occur are essentially two: cutting and crushing. Corpuscles that have fewer faces and therefore more acute or
"sharper" solid angles are smaller (assuming equilateral faces of
equal size) and better adept at cutting; those with more faces and
less acute solid angles are larger and so better at crushing. Thus
on contact of sufficient force, fire corpuscles, having the fewest
faces and therefore the sharpest edges, tend to disintegrate corpuscles of both air and water (as air does to water) by cutting. Similarly, water corpuscles, having the most faces and thus the most
obtuse edges, disintegrate corpuscles of both air and fire (as air
does to fire) by crushing. Thus an air corpuscle (eight faces) may
be cut (by fire) or crushed (by water) to be reconstituted as two
fire corpuscles (two times four faces). A water corpuscle (twenty
faces) may be cut (by fire or air) to be reconstituted as one corpuscle of fire (four faces) and two air corpuscles (two times eight
faces). Similarly, several fire corpuscles, say twenty (for a total of
eighty faces), may be crushed by water or air to be reconstituted
as, for example, five corpuscles of air (five times eight faces) and
two of water (two times twenty faces). Of course these three kinds
of corpuscles will also come into violent contact with corpuscles
of earth, whether cutting it or being crushed by it. In the former
case, the faces of earth corpuscles will break up only to recombine
with other faces of earth corpuscles to constitute new earth corpuscles. In the latter, earth acts as much as an agent of intertransformation among the other three as they themselves do.[144]
    This account raises the following question, which Plato antici-

---

144. Timaeus' examples of these intertransformations at 56c8–e7 allow for leaving
the equilateral triangular faces of the various corpuscles intact. We have seen that
these faces are themselves composed of two, six, eight, eighteen . . . elementary
half-equilaterals (Fig. 2). The breakup of these faces into their constituent half-
equilaterals does not figure in Plato's account of the intertransformation of fire,
earth, and water. But since, as was noted above, any transformation from one
kind to another will always be from a particular variety of one kind to one of
another (and difference of variety is a function of difference in "grade," i.e.,
number of half-equilaterals in an equilateral face), the breakup of the faces will
figure in the intertransformations as well.

pates. Suppose that some fire corpuscles jam against air corpuscles. What will determine whether the fire corpuscles will cut the air, rather than the air corpuscles crushing the fire? Timaeus' answer is that if corpuscles of one kind surround those of another kind (and therefore vastly outnumber them), the action of the surrounding one prevails. Thus air "surrounded" by fire will be subject to being cut up until all the air particles are reconstituted as fire. Air "surrounded" by water will be subject to being crushed until it is entirely transformed into water.

It is the agitation of the Receptacle that causes the corpuscles of the four kinds to collide with and so either cut or crush one another (57c2–6). Given the physical principle that that which surrounds assimilates to itself (by cutting or crushing) that which is surrounded, the result of these processes would eventually be the complete stratification of fire, air, and water (and earth?) into different regions of the universe, at which point the universe would be completely at rest. What, then, explains the continued compresence of the different kinds in the same regions of the universe, and hence the continued intertransformations?

To answer this question, Timaeus must first make the point that the corpuscles of each of the four kinds come in many different sizes, allowing for different grades or varieties of each. The size of a corpuscle is determined by the number of half-equilaterals that make up an equilateral face (57c7–d6). He must also account for motion and rest in terms of nonuniformity and uniformity (57d7–58a2). The spherical world, he says, "has a natural tendency to gather in upon itself" (58a6), leaving no gaps empty. Thus smaller corpuscles will tend to fill up gaps left between larger ones. Any gaps still left can only be filled by corpuscles still smaller. Ultimately fire, which has the smallest corpuscles, will fill up gaps within air and the others, as air will within water and earth, and water within earth. And since each of the kinds has a multiplicity of grades, the smallest grade of fire will be able to fill the smallest gaps. This compacting leaves each corpuscle exposed to the cutting edges or crushing surfaces of its neighbors, and the shaking of the Receptacle assures that the cutting and the crushing described earlier take place. The transformations that result bring about movement toward the kind's own region (from a state of nonuniformity to one of uniformity), but as the newly formed corpuscles move toward their like, new gaps emerge, which in turn are filled by smaller corpuscles, thus guaranteeing a perpetual state of nonuniformity.

(vi) The Varieties and Compounds of the Four Kinds
(58c5–61c2)

Timaeus concludes his account of the four primary bodies by sorting and describing the various varieties of fire, air, earth, and water, as well as their various compounds. Although the details need not detain us, the importance of the account should not be underestimated: it provides the link between the four primary bodies so far abstractly discussed, and the stuffs that make up the mid-sized objects of our everyday experience. These stuffs are in effect given a chemical analysis in terms of the two primitives of the system presented: the polyhedral shapes that distinguish the corpuscles of each of the four kinds, and the various size grades within each of the shapes. Some stuffs will be uniformly composed of a specific grade of a particular kind, some will be composed of two or more grades within a kind, and some will be composed of two or more grades of mixtures of two or more kinds, resulting in the possibility of "an infinite variety" of stuffs (57d3–6).

The three varieties of fire listed (flame, light, and glow) and the two of air (aether and mist) are each composed of uniformly sized triangles, though there are other "nameless" varieties composed of mixtures of various sizes. The multiple varieties of water are divided into two: the liquid and the liquifiable. Liquifiable waters include solids that when heated melt at a certain point. These are the varieties of metals.

The liquid waters are those which under normal conditions are fluid, a feature due to their composition out of small but unequally sized icosahedra. Liquifiable waters (metals) normally appear as solids, composed of larger and equally sized icosahedra. When heated, fire corpuscles (tetrahedra) penetrate these solids, cutting up the icosahedra into smaller and variously sized ones and rendering them fluid. When cooled, jelling takes place: the fire corpuscles are expelled, and the vacated spaces are filled (under pressure from the surrounding air) by the formation of larger and more uniformly sized icosahedra.

Waters in a fluid state, whether liquid or liquifiable, are actually compounds of water and fire. It is easy to see why this must be so in the case of molten metals. If the tetrahedra that cut the icosahedra to constitute smaller icosahedra in the process of melting were themselves transformed into icosahedra, there would be no fire to be expelled in the process of cooling, and jelling could not take place. But just as liquifiable waters in a fluid state are capable of jelling, so liquid waters in their normal state are capable of freezing, a process by which their constituent icosahedra are equalized and enlarged, and that process, too, must be due to the expulsion of fire. All waters, then, whether liquid or liquifiable, are capable of becoming liquid or solid in exactly the same ways, and so the distinction between liquid and liquifiable waters has no chemical basis; its basis lies simply in how these stuffs appear to us under normal conditions.[145]

After describing some examples of "saps," mixtures of several varieties of waters, Timaeus turns to the varieties of earth, of which there are basically four: (1) stone (earth from which all water has been expelled); (2) pottery (earth from which moisture has been expelled by fire); and lava (earth that is made liquifiable by fire); (3) soda and salt (varieties of earth that are the residue of much water and are soluble by water); and (4) glass and wax (compounds of earth and water that are soluble by fire but not by water). Timaeus gives an account only of the first and the last of these processes. In an earth-water mixture, he says, the water disintegrates into air (presumably the earth cubes "crush" the water icosahedra to form air octahedra), which escapes "toward its own region," putting pressure on the air surrounding the earth, which in turn compresses the earth to the point of rendering it impermeable by water or air. Similar analyses are probably presumed for the emergence of the next two varieties. But he clearly feels that a special explanation is required for the last: how can it be that some compounds of earth and water are soluble *only* by fire, and not by air or water?

Normally, he says, neither fire nor air will dissolve masses of earth. The earth cubes are large and tend to have big gaps between them, so that they are invulnerable to the cutting action of the fire tetrahedra or the air octahedra which pass through these gaps without jamming against the cubes. Only the water icosahedra, being larger, will jam against the cubes and undo them. But occasionally there will be masses of earth that are much more than normally "compressed." In those cases the gaps are very

---

145. We might wonder what it is that prevents the cutting action of the fire tetrahedra upon the water icosahedra from producing quite a number of octahedra (air corpuscles) in the process. Timaeus does not say. It could be that many of these *are* produced in the process but are eventually eliminated by the crushing action of the predominating icosahedra, and so their existence is only temporary.

small, so that only the fire corpuscles can pass through them, but
not without jamming against them, and so not without cutting
up the cubes. In general, sufficiently compressed quantities of
earth, water, or air can ultimately be broken up only by the cutting
action of fire. Given these physical principles, an earth-water
compound is insoluble by water if its water is tightly packed
within the gaps of earth. Fire, however, can enter this tightly
packed water and cut up some of the icosahedra (turning them
into air octahedra that escape to their "likes"?), giving the remaining icosahedra room to disperse the earth cubes, thereby rendering the water-earth compound fluid.

(vii) The Perceptual Properties of Sensible Objects (61c3–68d7)

In the final section of this part of the discourse, Timaeus turns to
giving an account of the perceptual properties possessed by the
physical objects constituted by the stuffs he has just finished
discussing. Such an account, he notes, presupposes an account
of the psychophysiology of sense perception, which he has not
yet developed. On the other hand, the latter sort of account no
less presupposes one of the perceptual properties of physical
objects. So he asks us to grant provisionally the existence of the
mortal soul and the body (both of which will be fully accounted
for in the third main section of the discourse—69a6–71e2 and
72d4–76e6 resp.).

The entire account is developed in two stages. From 61e3 to
65b3 Timaeus discusses the properties we discern through touch.
These include hot-cold (61d5–62b6), hard-soft (62b6–c3), heavy-
light (62c3–63e8, the latter couplet being explained by way of an
analysis of above-below), and smooth-rough (63e8–64a1). Since
we have no separate organ of touch, these properties are described
as having "a common effect upon the body as a whole" (64a2–3;
cf. "affect the whole body in a common way," 65b4). This stage
also includes an account of how these properties are perceived,
insofar as their perception causes us to feel pleasure or pain
(64a2–65b3). The second stage (65b4–68d7) discusses properties
perceived by our various sense organs: tastes (65c1–66c7: sour,
tangy, bitter, salty, pungent, acid, and sweet), odors (65d1–67a6:
not named but described as either pleasant or offensive), sounds
(67a7–c3: high and low pitched, smooth and rough, loud and

soft), and colors[146] (67c4–68d7: transparent, black and white, bright and brilliant, red and orange, purple, violet, gray, amber, beige, cobalt blue, turquoise and green).

The general theory of perception that underlies this account is developed in the subsection on pleasure and pain (64a2–65b3). Perception is produced by the action of an external object upon a perceiving subject, either upon any part of the subject's body as a whole or on a particular sense organ. The external object has certain perceptual "properties" (*pathēmata*), which are a function of the constitution of its primary triangles. The contact of the object, given its particular properties, produce a "disturbance" or "experience" (*pathos*)[147] in the subject's body. This disturbance may or may not be communicated to the subject's center of consciousness (*to phronimon*, 64b5), depending on the "mobility" of the subject's bodily parts. If the affected bodily parts are mobile (capable of being changed by the disturbance), then the disturbance originally created on the surface of the body (the skin or any of the sense organs) is relayed along a succession of interior bodily parts to the center of consciousness, and perception occurs. If they are not, that is, if they remain unchanged by the disturbance, the relay is either not begun or is left incomplete, and perception does not occur.

In this way, our perception of things as hot or cold, hard or soft, and smooth or rough can be accounted for. Timaeus' inclusion of "heavy" and "light" in this set is surprising, and his account of these properties sophisticated. While we may feel the hotness, hardness, or smoothness of an object with some part of our skin, our perception of their heaviness is not "felt" in the same way. So an account of heaviness and lightness requires more than

---

146. The range of properties perceived by sight includes but is not restricted to what we would recognize as colors.

147. Both *pathos* and *pathēma* are nouns derived from the verb *paschein*, to undergo, experience, or be affected. Although Plato tends to use *pathēma* to refer to a property of the external object that a subject perceives it to have (sweet, hard, etc.) and *pathos* for the affection (conscious or unconscious—where conscious, I translate "experience") undergone by the subject as a result of the action of the object on the percipient subject, his use of these two terms in this way is not always consistent. Thus at 64d6, 65b4, 66b6, and c6–7, Plato uses *pathēma* where terminological consistency would lead us to expect *pathos*, while at 63d4 (and possibly at 62b5) he does the opposite. Here and in the translation I ignore these exceptions.

a reference to the shapes and compactness of the constituent corpuscles of objects: it also requires reference to other physical properties, in this case the tendency of each of the four kinds to gather with its "likes" in its appropriate region of the universe. In speaking of these regions of the universe, Timaeus wants to deny that any is "above" or "below" any other in an absolute or "natural" sense. Above and below, and upward and downward, are all relative to the natural direction in which bodies of each of the four kinds move when unimpeded.[148] In absolute terms we can no more say that the region of fire is "above" that of air than the reverse. When the same force is exerted to move different amounts of fire into the region occupied by air, the smaller quantity "yields" more readily to the force applied. Similarly, when the same force is exerted to move different amounts of earth into the region of air, the smaller amount yields more easily. Both the fire and the earth are lighter to the extent that they yield more easily, and heavier to the extent that they yield less easily. In other words, the more force it takes to move a thing out of its own region into an alien region, the heavier it is. Its degree of heaviness is the degree of its tendency to move back into its proper region. "Above" and "below" should be redefined accordingly: the "home" region toward which a body moves unless impeded is always "below" it, and its movement toward that region is "downward," while its forced movement into an alien region is always an "upward" movement.[149]

Before leaving this section of the discourse, we should consider how Plato's physical account of the perceptual properties of things comports with his metaphysical account of objects and their properties earlier (49b–52d). There, we recall, a physical object is some particular part of the Receptacle characterized in a certain way by virtue of its participation in the relevant Form. A bit of fire there is a part of the Receptacle that appears fiery (51b4–5), just because that part of the Receptacle at that particular time participates in (copies, reflects, images) the Form of Fire. And for that bit of fire to be hot, or bright, is, similarly, for it to participate in the Forms of the Hot and the Bright. In the physical account just

---

148. And *not* relative to the center of the universe, as one might expect Timaeus to have said at this point (and is suggested by the image of one walking around the circumference of the sphere (63a2–4).

149. On this account, two balloons, one filled with helium (a form of fire, let's say) and one with water, will both travel "downward" when released in air.

given, a bit of fire is a constellation (primarily) of tetrahedra, and for it to be hot is for the edges of these tetrahedra to cut the bodies of the percipient subjects (61d5–62a5). For the fire to be bright is for it to pounce on the internal fire proceeding from our eyes as a "visual stream" (45b–d), a collision that dilates the eyes and produces tears that quench the invading fire (67e6–68b1). How can these accounts be reconciled?

Are these perceptual properties supervenient upon the physical constitutions of sensible objects, "laid over" them, so to speak, by their participation in Forms? If this were the case, the metaphysical and the physical accounts are distinct descriptions not of the same reality, but of different realities. A thing's softness, for instance, would then only be contingently and not essentially related to its physical composition, without any explanation of that relation. Plato gives us no encouragement, however, to think of properties in this way. The perceptual properties just *are* the states and activities of the thing's constituent polyhedra as these states and activities are experienced by a perceiving subject.[150] If this is the case, then physical objects and their properties may be explained in terms of two of Aristotle's four "causes," the formal cause and the material cause.[151] If, for example, we wish to know why this object is gold, we may answer from the formal point of view by saying that the part of the Receptacle that constitutes the object images the Form of Gold. But if we then ask further what it is about *this* Receptacle part (as opposed to some other) that enables it to do so, the answer will be in terms of the nature, size, and compactness of its constituent polyhedra: to be a gold object is to be made up of the finest and most uniform octahedra (59a8–b3).

C. The Cooperation of Intellect and Necessity: 69a6–92c9

The two foregoing sections of the discourse have laid the theoretical foundation for the present one. In this section, the primary theme is the psychophysical formation and constitution of human beings, and Timaeus will provide an account that focuses particularly on the purposes and mechanisms of the human body and its various parts, as well as the conditions that promote psychophysical well-being and its opposite. As he approaches the end

---

150. For a fuller discussion, see Kung [69], especially pp. 314–17.

151. Aristotle's account of the four "causes" is found at *Physics* 194b16–95a3.

of this part of the discourse, Timaeus brings to light its entire point, hinted at from time to time in his prior remarks: human beings are built for the attainment of virtue and wisdom, and thereby of happiness, though the risks and perils of achieving this are very great and difficult to overcome. For Plato, an account of the physics and the metaphysics of the world is anything but value-neutral. The whole account which from the beginning is, as we have seen, driven by aesthetic demands (p. xxxvii), concludes with an implicit exhortation to do what must be done to achieve a life of supreme happiness (90a2–d7).

The details of Timaeus' psychophysical account are fascinating and present a host of interesting questions about Plato's knowledge of human anatomy and the extent of his contribution to that science, which already in his day had generated a considerable literature.[152] I shall leave these questions aside to focus on how Timaeus dovetails considerations of teleology and necessity in his account, and the success and limitations of this project.

(i) The Creation of the Mortal Soul (69c5–72d3)

We saw that it was the craftsman himself who had created individual (initially human) souls, assigned them each to a home star, and "sown" them into the planets (41d4–42a3; above, p. lii). These souls were destined for incarnation, but the task of constructing the bodies to contain them was handed over to the created gods.[153] These gods begin by constructing the head to contain the soul, but a complete body is required as well, to convey the head from place to place (69c6–7, cf. 44d3–45b2). Before constructing these bodies, however, the lesser gods must create a soul of a different kind, to support sense perception, pleasure and pain, and the emotions (above, p. liii). This is the "mortal kind" of soul, which is divided into two parts. Its superior part is seated in the heart, and its inferior part in the belly.

The partitioning of the soul is recognizably similar to that of the *Republic*, but also different from it. In the *Republic*, the soul is a single entity, with three parts: Reason, Spirit, and Appetite. Its

---

152. These are the "Hippocratic" writings, a compilation—probably by multiple authors—of treatises written for the most part between 430 and 340 B.C.E. See Von Staden [99].

153. Throughout this part of the discourse, Timaeus will speak as often of "the god" (singular) as of "the gods" as the creator(s) of the body parts. The switch from plural to singular is particularly harsh in 71a.

immortality as a whole is never questioned.[154] In the *Timaeus*, however, there are two "kinds" (*eidē*) of soul, the immortal and the mortal. It is only the latter kind of soul that is here divisible into anything like parts, analogous to the division of parts in the *Republic*.[155]

The very existence of the mortal kind of soul and its susceptibility to the "dreadful disturbances" of pleasure and pain and the violent emotions that afflict the organism is, as we have seen, due to Necessity.[156] Like the soul of the world, an individual soul is to be embodied (in its case, in a head), but unlike it, it has an external environment to contend with, so that it needs a "carriage" (the rest of the body, limbs, etc.) to get from place to place, and sense perception to direct that carriage and become aware of friendly and hostile objects to encounter or avoid. Pleasure and pain are consequences of sense perception,[157] and the strong emotions are reactions to pleasure and pain. These emotions, we have seen (above, p. liii) disturb the regular motions of the soul, resulting in moral degeneration and biological devolution if they are not mastered. Here already we encounter a conflict between Intellect and Necessity: Given the creation of a maximally beautiful and good world, it is not possible to create individual living things without an external environment, hence without sense perception, pleasure and pain, and their concomitant violent emotions. Or, to sum it up, given such a world, it is not possible to create living things not susceptible to moral degeneration.

The two mortal parts of the soul are seated in specific bodily organs, each of which is constructed so as to render it suitable to its particular task. Thus the heart, because it is the center of the circulatory system, which reaches all the bodily parts, is particularly suited to enable Spirit to subdue on behalf of Reason the "wrongful acts" of Appetite anywhere in the body. And the lungs' softness and inflatability, in turn, serve to relieve the pounding of the heart and keep it cool (70a2–d6). Similarly, Appetite is

---

154. See Robinson [37], pp. 50–54, who criticizes other views.

155. Timaeus gives no account of the origin of the mortal kind of soul. If its origin is distinct from that of the immortal kind, it is something of a mystery what it is made out of: apparently not of the residue of soul-stuff, out of which the craftsman had made the immortal soul, nor of the four primary bodies, out of which the body is made. Possibly the creators "made" mortal souls by adapting the immortal souls to some degree to carry out the functions required by embodied existence.

156. N. 115 above.

157. Plato tends to treat pleasure and pain as themselves sensations.

made to live as far away from Reason as possible and gorge itself
in the belly, which is shaped like a feeding trough for that purpose,
and the glistening surface of the liver serves to act as a mirror
relaying dreadful images sent down by Reason which, assisted
by excretions of the liver's bitterness, frighten Appetite into sub-
mission.[158] And the spleen has a spongy nature, suited for wiping
the surface of the liver, absorbing in itself like a dust cloth the
latter's impurities and keeping it clean and bright (72c1–d3).

(ii) The Creation of the Body Parts and Systems (72d4–81e5)

The cooperation of Intellect with Necessity is also evident in the
formation of the body parts. Our intestines serve to store the
excesses of food and drink we consume due to our lack of discipline. Were it not for the long coil of our lower alimentary tract,
we would need to consume food and drink constantly, thus keeping us from the pursuit of philosophy and of the arts (72e7–73a8).
Bone is created to protect the marrow, sinews and flesh to protect
the bone, and skin to protect the flesh. The purpose of the marrow
is to anchor the soul to the body, and so it must be composed of
exceptionally fine triangles (73b1–c3). The brain of an animal is
that mass or marrow to which the immortal soul is anchored,
and it is encased by the skull; the remaining marrow anchors the
mortal parts of the soul, and is enclosed by the bones (c6–e1).
The skull and bones are baked by the god(s) to a hardness that
serves their function (e1–5). Similarly, sinews and flesh, necessary
to preserve the integrity of the bones, are distributed over the
skeleton in such a way as to allow joints to flex and bones which
contain more marrow (soul) than others to be more sensitive
(74a7–e1).

The whole account (which includes, besides the above, also
the formation of the mouth and its parts [75d5–e5], skin [e5–76b1],
hair [b1–d3], and nails [e6]) has—though often not explicitly—a
uniform structure: all the body parts are made out of such and
such material (mixtures in particular proportions of earth, water,
air, and fire) so as to possess such and such characteristics (hard,
soft, porous, malleable, etc.), which enable them to perform such
and such functions (to protect another body part, to support

---

158. The liver also has a further function which seems to fascinate Timaeus
(71e2–72d3), that of divination.

the functioning of another part, etc.), functions that in turn are subservient to certain purposes (to enable the living thing to walk erect, to move about in certain ways, to perceive its environment, etc.), and, ultimately, to the final purpose of the living thing's existence, which is the pursuit and preservation of virtue, wisdom, and happiness. The material composition of these parts, and the characteristics they have in virtue of that composition, are determined by Necessity. The triumph of Intellect over Necessity consists in the selection and shaping of just these parts to accomplish just those purposes.

At the same time, Necessity sometimes imposes a constraint on Intellect. This constraint is most clearly in evidence in Timaeus' discussion of the degree of thickness of flesh around those bones (or bone parts) that contain the most marrow (74e1–75c7). Intellect requires that those bones of the human skeleton which contain greater amounts of marrow be denser and protected by a greater covering of flesh than bones which do not. Since the head is the container of the brain-marrow (73d), it ought accordingly to be made of dense bone and covered by a thick layer of flesh. On the other hand, Intellect also requires that marrow be responsive to sensation, but massive amounts of bone and flesh would impede this. Since it is better to permit the marrow to be maximally responsive than to be maximally protected, a concession must be made to Necessity, and the first of these requirements must yield to the second: longevity must yield to sensitivity and intelligence. By and large, however, Intellect succeeds in making Necessity serve its purposes: not only the parts of the body, but also the circulation, respiratory, and digestive systems are explained in accordance with these principles.

Before embarking on a discussion of the various systems of the human body (digestive, respiratory, and circulatory), Timaeus gives an account of how living things are to be nourished. They are to feed on plants,[159] which themselves have a claim to being called "living things" (77b1–3; see tr. note 87), insofar as they possess the lower part of the mortal soul (Appetite). To that extent, plants have a limited capacity for sensation and desire, pleasure and pain (b3–6), and so they count, if only very minimally, as "animals."

The account of the digestive, respiratory, and circulation

---

159. The passage carries no implication for vegetarianism. Nonhuman animals have yet to "devolve" (91d6 *ff.*).

systems is strange to modern ears. Timaeus treats all three as integrated aspects of a single system, which he calls the "irrigation" system. This system consists of components, and a mechanism that drives the components. The components of the system are the belly, into which food and drink descends, and the blood vessels. Digestion converts the food and drink into blood, which is circulated throughout the body by the blood vessels to nourish the entire body. Two major blood veins stretch along the length of the back, on either side of the spine, and these function as the primary conduits for passing the blood on to the network of subsidiary blood vessels throughout the body. Timaeus must explain how food and drink, which descend into the belly, are converted into blood and are transported from the belly to the two primary veins. The mechanism that drives this process is respiration, of which Timaeus gives an account strictly in terms of the physics of the primary bodies (fire, air, water, and earth) involved, given the principle that a vacuum does not exist. The main lines of the account are as follows.

Timaeus begins by laying down the physical principle that "whatever is made up of smaller parts holds in larger parts, while whatever consists of larger parts is incapable of holding in smaller parts" (78a2–3). The wall of the belly cannot be penetrated by food and drink, but can be penetrated by fire and air. To conduct the contents of the belly ("moisture" 78b3, digested food and drink converted to blood) from the belly to the two primary veins, something that is able to "hold in" this moisture will be required, and that something can consist only of fire and air. Timaeus compares the way this is supposed to work to a fish trap. A fish trap has an outer shell and an inner structure that provides a one-way passage for fish (often by way of a funnel) into the interior of the trap. In the same way, Timaeus invites us to imagine an outer "shell" of air enclosing an interior fabric of fire. The air is able to enter and exit from the body by way of the "pores" that allow passage, but it may also enter and exit by way of (one of)[160] the "funnels" that line our trachea and esophagus. Whenever air exits the body by one of these ways, it causes other air to enter by way of the other: for example, air that is exhaled puts pressure on the air that surrounds the body, pushing and eventually displacing an equal amount of air that simultaneously enters our

---

160. Presumably the one lining the trachea, the only "funnel" involved in respiration.

bodies through the pores. Likewise, air that is inhaled displaces air already inside our bodies, pushing it out through the pores. This mechanism of pressure and displacement is often referred to as the "circular thrust."[161]

We might wonder what it is that prevents respiration from being a perpetual one-way process—perpetual inhalation, say, with concomitant perpetual expulsion of air through the pores. What is it that accounts instead for the oscillating process familiar to us? The answer Timaeus gives to this question is far from clear. Because the interior of the body is hot, air gets heated (combined with fire) the farther into the body it gets, and cooled the farther away from the body's center it gets. Relying on the principle that what is hot seeks to move toward its own region (79d5–6), Timaeus maintains that air that has entered through the body's pores and become hot will have a tendency to depart the way it came, and so also air that has entered through the trachea. But just why it has that tendency is difficult to see.[162]

How do these mechanics explain the transportation of the digested food—now newly formed blood—from the belly to the primary veins? We can now see how the air, entering through the body's pores and becoming heated, can penetrate into the belly, its fire dissolve the belly's contents and transport that content through the passages through which it travels on its way farther into or out of the body toward the two primary veins. Digestion, then, is a by-product of respiration, itself explicable strictly in terms of physical principles. Once again, Intellect succeeds in making a virtue of Necessity.

Timaeus concludes his account of the digestive system with an explanation of how nourishment takes place. Blood is simply the liquid that is the product of fire's cutting of the ingested food particles. Its function is to "replenish" the "depleted areas" of the body. The body is subject to continual depletion or disintegration, as its constituent fire, etc., tends to move toward its own region of the universe. Depleted areas are replenished by the fire, etc., corpuscles of the blood, as here, too, like joins with like. The body will grow as long as the rate of replenishment exceeds that of depletion; it will diminish if the reverse is the case. Growth takes

---

161. Timaeus will go on to mention parenthetically several other contexts in which this mechanism is operative: "medical cupping," swallowing, projectile motion, and others (79e10–80c8).

162. See Taylor [39], pp. 562–66.

place in young living things, because the triangles of their body parts successfully break up and so assimilate those of the blood. In old age, the body's triangles more often succumb to those of the blood, and the living thing declines, eventually to the point that the marrow triangles become undone and the soul departs from the body.

(iii) Diseases of the Body and the Soul (81e6–87b9)

The mention of the aging process and natural death serves to introduce a discussion of the origin of diseases of the body. The classification of various originating causes of diseases owes much to recent and contemporary medical literature.[163] One class of diseases is caused by an imbalance of fire, air, water, or earth in the body, or by their movements out of their own regions, and so on. Timaeus does not speculate about the causes of these "unnatural" (82a7) phenomena. These are no doubt the effects of the residual random motions of the Receptacle, and as such are the products of Necessity over which Intellect has no power to prevail. Another class consists of diseases that are specific to the organs and tissues ("secondary structures"). These are caused by a reversal of the process of nutrition. Flesh and sinew, for example, are derived from and nourished by different parts of blood. When they waste away, they discharge their wastes back into the bloodstream, contaminating it in various ways. The waste products disturb the natural flow of blood and attack other tissues and organs. The disintegrating flesh produces a variety of "humors"— bile, serum, and phlegm, each of which has its own subvarieties, described by Timaeus in graphic detail. A more serious condition arises when the oily substance that glues the flesh to the bone is corrupted. Flesh and bone become detached from each other and from the sinews, and the flesh is dissolved in the bloodstream. Still more serious is the disintegration of diseased bone and its dissolution back into the bloodstream. Most serious of all, and certainly fatal, is the spread of disease to the marrow.

A third class of diseases is caused by blockages in the body of air (either breathed in or formed in the body by decomposing flesh) and of two of the "humors," phlegm and bile. Collectively, these conditions cause a great variety of diseases (including epi-

---

163. His debts to Philistion of Locri and possibly to Diocles of Carystus are described by Cornford [14], pp. 333–36.

lepsy, the "sacred disease")[164] and bring excruciating pain, along with fevers and inflammations of various sorts.

From a classification of diseases of the body, Timaeus proceeds to give a brief account of diseases of the soul, at least of those that arise from a bodily condition. Psychic disease is always a form of "mindlessness" (*anoia*, absence of *nous*), of which there are two kinds: madness and ignorance. Excessive physical pleasure and pain produce madness. In the case of intense pleasures (and here Timaeus is thinking primarily of excessive sexual indulgence), there is a purely physiological cause: the marrow produces an overabundance of seed, which flows out through the pores in the bones, moistening the whole body and leading to sexual overindulgence. In the case of severe pains—brought on, for example, by physical disease—the motions of the soul are disturbed, particularly as each of the three physical regions of the soul is affected.

The madness of sexual overindulgence and other pathologies due to excessive pleasure is a condition that is not morally blameworthy, and people should not be reproached for it, "for no one is willfully bad" (86d7–e1). This stark explanation seems to be a reprise of a doctrine found in Plato's early dialogues, known as the Socratic Paradox, and Plato's commitment or lack of it to this doctrine in his middle period and later work has been much discussed. We need not read it here as having the full import of the Socratic doctrine, which is essentially the claim that knowledge is sufficient for virtue, a claim that Plato implicitly denies in the *Republic*.[165] In the present context, Timaeus invokes it only to assert that when it is clear that one's mad and hence bad behavior is the result of psychophysical causes, that behavior is not willed or chosen, and thus it is inappropriate to hold the agent responsible for it. He does not assert that all behavior is due to such causes, or deny that in the presumed absence of such causes we are justified in holding people responsible for their actions. The same holds for the madness and badness caused by an excess of pain. Disease produces bad dispositions: bad temper, melancholy, recklessness, cowardice, forgetfulness, and stupidity (87a5–7). In a bad social environment devoid of intellectual pursuits, these

---

164. So called because it was popularly thought to be of supernatural origin, a view attacked by the (Hippocratic) author of *On the Sacred Disease*.

165. Compare *Rep.* IV, 436a *ff.*, which permits conflicts among the three parts of the soul which on occasion Appetite wins, as the story of Leontius (439e–440a) shows.

dispositions are not countered and are expressed in the corresponding behavior. Again, Timaeus absolves such agents of responsibility: they are victims of social and intellectual conditions not of their own making. Nevertheless, he urges, "one should make every possible effort to flee from badness . . . and to seize its opposite" (87b6–8), an appeal that would make little sense if he thought that all behavior is psychophysically or socially determined.

(iv) The Conditions and Causes of Psychophysical Well-being 87c1–90d7

The account of physical and psychic illnesses serves as a foil to the topic of the well-being of body and soul. Relying on the aesthetic principle basic to the entire cosmology, that "all that is good is beautiful and what is beautiful is . . . well-proportioned (87c4–6)," Timaeus begins by recommending a well-proportioned relationship between one's body and one's soul: a soul that is too vigorous for the body wears it out and makes it susceptible to disease, while a body that is too vigorous for the soul will lead one to pursue bodily desires (for food, drink, and sex, etc.) at the expense of those of the soul (for wisdom), resulting in the mental defect of ignorance. The remedy for both kinds of disproportion is the same: exercise. The mentally strong but physically frail should take care to exercise his body, while the physically robust but intellectually deficient should turn to study of the arts and the pursuit of wisdom.

Physical exercise ought to be modeled on the movement of the world brought on by the shaking action of the Receptacle: one's body is heated and cooled, moistened and dried, by the movements of things internal and external to it. Since good health consists of the proper proportions of these two sets of opposites, these movements must be maintained by moderate exercise. Exercise is the best way to induce motion in the body, since the motion is self-originating. Inferior to it is motion induced from without, in a conveyance like a boat that produces swaying or rocking. The worst kind of induced motion is that in which the body is entirely passive, such as medical purging by means of drugs. Treatment of illnesses by means of drugs, says Timaeus, should be avoided if at all possible. Diseases, like the organisms they inhabit, have a finite life span and will eventually run their course.

Drugs interfere with this process and tend to aggravate mild diseases or make one more susceptible to future recurrences of the disease.

It is, however, the exercise of the soul that is of highest priority. Each type of soul—the immortal and the two parts of the mortal soul—has its own motions,[166] which must be maintained in a relationship of proportionality to one another. Timaeus focuses exclusively, however, on the motions of the immortal soul, and his exhortation to "redirect the revolutions in our heads . . . by coming to learn the harmonies and revolutions of the universe" in order to achieve "that most excellent life offered to humankind by the gods, both now and forevermore (90d1–7)" is the climax of his discourse. But it raises an important question: how, we wonder, does the study of the mathematical structure of the world redirect those revolutions of our rational souls, enabling us to achieve that life of supreme excellence?

It should be recalled that prior to their incarnations, individual immortal souls are themselves, like the soul of the world, systems of geometrical and harmonic proportions (36a–b), systems that were violently disrupted at their incarnation by their encounter with the tides of nourishment and the disturbances of sense perception (43a–4a, esp. 43d). To restore these systems to their original state, time, proper education, and nurture are required (44b–c). Timaeus' present comment emphasizes the role of education in this process, and we are no doubt meant to recall the elaborate discussion of the philosopher-king's education in the *Republic*, Book 7, which includes geometry (plane and solid), astronomy (mathematical, not empirical), and harmonics. How does an immersion in these studies, leading to an understanding of the mathematical principles according to which the finished world operates, effect the regulation of the motions in the soul of the student? And how does that regulation in turn bring about his or her happiness?

The study Timaeus recommends is in fact the study of the constitution and operation of the soul of the world. When these become the object of study by one's own rational soul, the subject of the study, there is in effect an encounter or contact between

---

166. The immortal soul, made out of the same stuff as the soul of the world, shares in its motions, those of the Same and the Different. What the motions of the two mortal parts of the soul are, we are not told.

two "substances" of like nature, the macro-substance of the universal soul and the micro-substance of one's individual soul.[167] It is not unreasonable to suppose that Plato thinks that some sort of assimilation is effected by this contact, resulting in the conformity of the smaller to the larger. And once the motions of one's rational soul have been reconformed to those of the universal soul, one's soul has resumed the happy condition it was in prior to its incarnation and is thus fit to return eventually to its home star.

(v) The Creation of Women and Nonhuman Animals (90e1–92c3)

Although Timaeus has now reached the climax of his creation story, he has not quite reached the end. Of the four kinds of living things the world is to contain (39e10–40a2), only the "heavenly race of gods" and male human beings have so far been created. If the world is to be complete in its likeness to its eternal model, provision must be made for the creation of female human beings and airborne, land, and aquatic animals as well.

"All male-born humans who lived lives of cowardice and injustice were reborn in the second generation as women" (90e6–91a1).[168] With the generation of women, human reproduction is now possible, and Timaeus accounts for sexual desire by postulating an ensouled "living thing" within both the male and the female anatomies. This living thing inside us is our reproductive system, which is credited with desires of its own—desires that are pent up until they are released and satisfied in the act of procreation. Sexual desire, then, is not a desire of the male or female proper—not even of the appetitive part of his or her soul—but of the reproductive organs. In this way Timaeus explains the "unruly and self-willed" (91b5–6) character of sexual desire.

The division of nonhuman animals into three classes is explained in terms of degrees of human failure to properly restore the soul. Birds are reincarnations of "innocent but simpleminded" souls that had studied the heavens empirically instead of mathematically (91d6–e1). Though they exercised their rational souls,

---

167. Plato regularly thinks of coming to know or understand an object as coming into some sort of psychic contact with it. See, for example, *Phaedo* 65b9, 79d6.

168. Plato's views on women are controversial and the subject of much ongoing debate. For some bibliographical material, see Vlastos [98] note *ad finem*. We are not told how, "in the second generation," female human beings could arrive on the scene, apparently without the instrumentality of any reproductive activity.

they did so wrongly. Land animals are descended from those who failed to exercise their reason at all and who instead followed the lead of the lower parts of the soul. The structure of their anatomies reflects the bent of their souls. And finally, aquatic animals "came from those men who were . . . the most stupid and ignorant of all" (92b1–2).

The emergence, then, of human females is due to (male) human moral failure, and the emergence of nonhuman animals to human intellectual failure. On the other hand, the complete likeness of the world to its eternal model requires the creation of all four kinds of living things. This presents a problem of theodicy in the *Timaeus* of which Plato shows no sign of being aware: the existence of these living things is demanded by the requirement that the world be as excellent as possible, yet is the unfortunate result of human failure. Would Plato have followed Leibniz in declaring that that failure, then, too, is demanded by the requirement of maximal excellence?[169]

The account is now formally concluded (92c4–9) with a statement of the task that has been accomplished. That was to describe and explain the creation of a world that is a visible image of an intelligible Living Thing (30c–d, 39e), reflecting its completeness, uniqueness, and supreme excellence. It will be left to generations of readers to come to debate how successful Timaeus has been in completing that task.

---

169. G. W. Leibniz, *Theodicy*. English translation by E. M. Huggard. Indianapolis: Bobbs Merrill, 1966.

ANALYTICAL TABLE OF CONTENTS

Introductory Conversation (17a1–27d4)

Timaeus' Discourse (27d5–92c9)

Prologue to the Discourse: 27d5–29d6

The Craftsmanship of Intellect: 29d7–47e2

THE EFFECTS OF NECESSITY: 47e3–69a5

The Cooperation of Intellect and Necessity in the Psychophysical Formation of Man and Other Living Things: 69a6–92c9

TIMAEUS

SOCRATES: One, two, three . . . Where's number four, Timaeus?
The four of you were my guests yesterday and today I'm to
be yours.[1]

TIMAEUS: He came down with something or other, Socrates.
He wouldn't have missed our meeting willingly.

SOCRATES: Well then, isn't it for you and your companions to
fill in for your absent friend?

TIMAEUS: You're quite right. Anyhow, we'll do our best not *b*
to come up short. You did such a fine job yesterday hosting us
visitors that now it wouldn't be right if the three of us didn't go
all out to give you a feast in return.

SOCRATES: Do you remember all the subjects I assigned to you
to speak on?

TIMAEUS: Some we do. And if there are any we don't—well,
you're here to remind us. Better still, if it's not too much trouble,
why don't you take a moment to go back through them from the
beginning? That way they'll be the more firmly fixed in our minds.

SOCRATES: Very well. I talked about politics yesterday and my *c*
main point, I think, had to do with the kind of political structure
cities should have and the kind of men that should make it up
so as to be the best possible.[2]

TIMAEUS: Yes, Socrates, so you did, and we were all very
satisfied with your description of it.

---

1. The conversation is presumably taking place at the celebration of the Panathen-
aic Festival in Athens (cf. 21a). The festival was an annual event; the Great Panathenaea, a more elaborate celebration, took place once every four years.
2. The construction here follows that proposed by Fraccaroli, rejected by Taylor
(Taylor [39], p. 46).

SOCRATES: Didn't we begin by separating off the class of farmers and all the other craftsmen in the city from the class of those who were to wage war on its behalf?

TIMAEUS: Yes.

d SOCRATES: And we followed nature in giving each person only one occupation, one craft for which he was well suited. And so we said that only those whose job it was to wage war on everyone's behalf should be the guardians of the city. And if some foreigner or even a citizen were to go against the city to cause
18 trouble, these guardians should judge their own subjects lightly, since they are their natural friends. But they should be harsh, we said, with the enemies they encountered on the battlefield.

TIMAEUS: Yes, absolutely.

SOCRATES: That's because—as I think we said—the guardians' souls should have a nature that is at once both spirited and philosophical to the highest degree, to enable them to be appropriately gentle or harsh as the case may be.

TIMAEUS: Yes.

SOCRATES: What about their training? Didn't we say that they were to be given both physical and cultural training, as well as training in any other appropriate fields of learning?

TIMAEUS: We certainly did.

b SOCRATES: Yes, and we said, I think, that those who received this training shouldn't consider gold or silver or anything else as their own private property. Like the professionals they are, they should receive from those under their protection a wage for their guardianship that's in keeping with their moderate way of life. And we said that they should share their expenses and spend their time together, live in one another's company, and devote their care above all to excellence, now that they were relieved of all other occupations.

TIMAEUS: Yes, we said that as well.

SOCRATES: And in fact we even made mention of women. We *c* said that their natures should be made to correspond with those of men, and that all occupations, whether having to do with war or with the other aspects of life, should be common to both men and women.

TIMAEUS: That, too, was discussed.

SOCRATES: And what did we say about the procreation of children? We couldn't possibly forget that subject, because what we said about it was so unusual. We decided that they should all have spouses and children in common and that schemes should be devised to prevent any one of them from recognizing his or her own particular child. Every one of them would believe that *d* they all make up a single family, and that all who fall within their own age bracket are their sisters and brothers, that those who are older, who fall in an earlier bracket, are their parents or grandparents, while those who fall in a later one are their children or grandchildren.

TIMAEUS: You're right. That really was an unforgettable point.

SOCRATES: And surely we also remember saying, don't we, that to make their natures as excellent as possible right from the start, the rulers, male and female, should secretly arrange marriages by lot, to make sure that good men and bad ones *e* would each as a group be separately matched up with women like themselves? And we said that this arrangement wouldn't create any animosity among them, because they'd believe that the matching was due to chance?

TIMAEUS: Yes, we remember.

SOCRATES: And do we also remember saying that the children *19* of the good parents were to be brought up, while those of the bad ones were to be secretly handed on to another city? And that these children should be constantly watched as they grew up, so that the ones that turned out deserving might be taken back again and the ones they kept who did not turn out that way should change places with them?

TIMAEUS: We did say so.

SOCRATES: So now, Timaeus, are we done with our review of yesterday's talk—at least with its main points—or are we missing some point we made then? Have we left anything out?

b   TIMAEUS: Not a thing, Socrates. This is exactly what we said.[3]

SOCRATES: All right, I'd like to go on now and tell you what I've come to feel about the political structure we've described. My feelings are like those of a man who gazes upon magnificent-looking animals, whether they're animals in a painting or even alive but standing still, and who then finds himself eager to look at them in motion or engaged in some struggle or conflict that
c seems to show off their distinctive physical qualities. I felt the same thing about the city we've described. I'd love to listen to someone give a speech depicting our city in a contest with other cities, competing for those prizes that cities typically compete for. I'd love to see our city distinguish itself in the way it goes to war and in the way it pursues the war: that it deals with the other cities, one after another, in ways that reflect positively on its own education and training, both in word and deed—that is, both in how it behaves toward them and how it negotiates with them.
d Now on these matters, Critias and Hermocrates, I charge myself with being quite unable to sing fitting praise to our city and its men. That this should be so in my case isn't at all surprising. But I have come to have the same opinion of the poets, our ancient poets as well as today's. I have no disrespect for poets in general, but everyone knows that imitators as a breed are best and most adept at imitating the sorts of things they've been trained to imitate. It's difficult enough for any one of them to do a decent
e job of imitating in performance, let alone in narrative description, anything that lies outside their training. And again, I've always thought that sophists as a class are very well versed in making long speeches and doing many other fine things. But because they wander from one city to the next and never settle down in homes of their own, I'm afraid their representations of those philosopher-statesmen would simply miss the mark. Sophists are bound to misrepresent whatever these leaders accomplish on the battlefield when they engage any of their enemies, whether in actual warfare or in negotiations.

---

3. For the relation of this summary to the political philosophy of the *Republic*, see the Introduction, pp. xxvi–xxvii.

So that leaves people of your sort, then. By nature as well as by training you take part in both philosophy and politics at once. Take Timaeus here. He's from Locri, an Italian city under the rule 20 of excellent laws. None of his compatriots outrank him in property or birth, and he has come to occupy positions of supreme authority and honor in his city. Moreover, he has, in my judgment, mastered the entire field of philosophy. As for Critias, I'm sure that all of us here in Athens know that he's no mere layman in any of the areas we're talking about. And many people whose testimony must surely be believed assure us that Hermocrates, too, is well qualified by nature and training to deal with these matters. Al- b ready yesterday I was aware of this when you asked me to discuss matters of government, and that's why I was eager to do your bidding. I knew that if you'd agree to make the follow-up speech, no one could do a better job than you. No one today besides you could present our city pursuing a war in a way that reflects her true character. Only you could give her all she requires. So now that I'm done speaking on my assigned subject, I've turned the tables and assigned you to speak on the subject I've just described. You've thought about this together as a group, and you've agreed c to reciprocate at this time. Your speeches are your hospitality gifts, and so here I am, all dressed up for the occasion. No one could be more prepared to receive your gifts than I.

HERMOCRATES: Yes indeed, Socrates, you won't find us short on enthusiasm, as Timaeus has already told you. We don't have the slightest excuse for not doing as you say. Why, already yesterday, right after we had left here and got to Critias' guest quarters, where we're staying—and even earlier on our way there—we were thinking about this very thing. And then Critias brought d up a story that goes way back. Tell him the story now, Critias, so he can help us decide whether or not it will serve the purpose of our assignment.

CRITIAS: Yes, we really should, if our third partner, Timaeus, also agrees.

TIMAEUS: Of course I do.

CRITIAS: Let me tell you this story then, Socrates. It's a very strange one, but even so, every word of it is true. It's a story that *e* Solon, the wisest of the seven sages, once vouched for.[4] He was a kinsman and a very close friend of my great-grandfather Dropides. Solon himself says as much in many places in his poetry. Well, Dropides told the story to my grandfather Critias, and the old man in his turn would tell it to us from memory. The story is that our city had performed great and marvelous deeds in ancient times, which, owing to the passage of time and to the destruction of human life, have vanished. Of all these deeds, one

21 in particular was magnificent. It is this one that we should now do well to commemorate and present to you as our gift of thanks. In so doing we shall also offer the goddess a hymn, as it were, of just and true praise on this her festival.[5]

SOCRATES: Splendid! Tell me, though, what was that ancient deed our city performed, the one that Solon reported and old Critias told you about? I've never heard of it. They say it really happened?

CRITIAS: I'll tell you. It's an ancient story I heard from a man who was no youngster himself. In fact, at the time Critias was

b pretty close to ninety years old already—so he said—and I was around ten. As it happened, it was the day of the presentation of children during the Apaturia.[6] On this occasion, as on others like it, we children got the customary treatment at the feast: our fathers started a recitation contest. Many compositions by many different poets were recited, and many of us children got to sing the verses of Solon, because they were new at the time. Now

c someone, a member of our clan, said that he thought that Solon was not only the wisest of men in general, but that his poetry in particular showed him to be the most civilized of all the poets. (The man may have been speaking his mind, or else he may just have wanted to make Critias feel good.) And the old man—how well I remember it—was tickled. He grinned broadly and said,

---

4. Solon (fl. early sixth century B.C.E.) was the author of significant social and political reforms, many of which paved the way for the development of Athenian democracy in the next century. The story of Solon's encounter with the Egyptian priests, and the Atlantis story related to him by the priests, are not attested anywhere before Plato, and are probably Plato's own invention. See the Introduction, pp. xxvii–xxviii.

5. The goddess is Athena, patron deity of Athens.

6. The Apaturia, an Ionian festival, was celebrated in Athens in October-November of each year. The presentation of children took place on the third day.

"Yes, Amynander, it's too bad that Solon wrote poetry only as a diversion and didn't seriously work at it like the other poets. And too bad that he never finished the story he'd brought back home with him from Egypt. He was forced to abandon that story on account of the civil conflicts and all the other troubles he found here when he returned. Otherwise not even Hesiod or Homer, *d* or any other poet at all, would ever have become more famous than he. That's what *I* think, anyhow." "Well, Critias? What story was that?" asked the other. "It's the story about the most magnificent thing our city has ever done," replied old Critias, "an accomplishment that deserves to be known far better than any of her other achievements. But owing to the march of time and because the men who accomplished it have perished, the story has not survived to the present." "Please tell us from the beginning," said the other. "What was this 'true story' that Solon heard? How did he get to hear it? Who told him?"

"In Egypt," Critias began, "in that part of the Delta where the *e* stream of the Nile divides around the vertex, there is a district called the Saitic. The most important city of this district is Sais. (This is also the city from which King Amasis came.) This city was founded by a goddess whose name was Neith in Egyptian and (according to the people there) Athena in Greek. The inhabitants are very friendly to Athens and claim to be related to our people somehow or other. Now Solon said that when he arrived there the people began to revere him. Further, he said that when 22 he asked those priests of theirs who were scholars of antiquity about ancient times, he discovered that just about every Greek, including himself, was all but completely ignorant about such matters. On one occasion, wanting to lead them on to talk about antiquity, he broached the subject of our own ancient history. He started talking about Phoroneus—the first human being, it is said—and about Niobe, and then he told the story of how Deucalion and Pyrrha survived the flood.[7] He went on to trace the lines *b* of descent of their posterity, and tried to compute their dates by calculating the number of years that had elapsed since the events of which he spoke. And then one of the priests, a very old man,

---

7. Phoroneus and Niobe were the children of the river Inachus; some ancient writers regarded Phoroneus as the "first man." Deucalion and Pyrrha were the survivors of the most recent flood (cf. 23b). The response of the old priest challenges Solon's mythological account and genealogical calculations of the events of antiquity with a historical and scientific account.

said, 'Ah, Solon, Solon, you Greeks are ever children. There isn't
an old man among you.' On hearing this, Solon said, 'What? What
do you mean?' 'You are young,' the old priest replied, 'young in
soul, every one of you. Your souls are devoid of beliefs about
antiquity handed down by ancient tradition. Your souls lack any
c learning made hoary by time. The reason for that is this: There
have been, and there will continue to be, numerous disasters that
have destroyed human life in many ways. The most serious of
these involve fire and water, while the lesser ones have numerous
other causes. And so also among your people the tale is told that
Phaethon, child of the Sun, once harnessed his father's chariot
but was unable to drive it along his father's course. He ended up
burning everything on the earth's surface and was destroyed
himself when a lightning bolt struck him. This tale is told as a
d myth, but the truth behind it is that there is a deviation in the
heavenly bodies that travel around the earth, which causes huge
fires that destroy what is on the earth across vast stretches of
time. When this happens, all those people who live in mountains
or in places that are high and dry are much more likely to perish
than the ones who live next to rivers or by the sea. Our Nile,
always our savior, is released[8] and at such times, too, saves us
from this disaster. On the other hand, whenever the gods send
floods of water upon the earth to purge it, the herdsmen and
shepherds in the mountains preserve their lives, while those who
e live in cities, in your region, are swept by the rivers into the sea.
But here, in this place, water does not flow from on high onto
our fields, at such a time or any other. On the contrary, its nature
is always to rise up from below. This, then, explains why the
antiquities preserved here are said to be the most ancient. The
truth is that in all places where neither inordinate cold nor heat
23 prevents it, the human race will continue to exist, sometimes in
greater, sometimes in lesser, numbers. Now of all the events
reported to us, no matter where they've occurred—in your parts
or in ours—if there are any that are noble or great or distinguished
in some other way, they've all been inscribed here in our temples
and preserved from antiquity on. In your case, on the other hand,
as in that of others, no sooner have you achieved literacy and all
the other resources that cities require, than there again, after the
usual number of years, comes the heavenly flood. It sweeps upon
b you like a plague, and leaves only your illiterate and uncultured

---

8. On the "release" of the Nile, see Cornford [14], 365–66.

people behind. You become infants all over again, as it were, completely unfamiliar with anything there was in ancient times, whether here or in your own region. And so, Solon, the account you just gave of your people's lineage is just like a nursery tale. First of all, you people remember only one flood, though in fact there had been a great many before. Second, you are unaware that the finest and best of all the races of humankind once lived in your region. This is the race from whom you yourself, your whole city, all that you and your countrymen have today, are *c* sprung, thanks to the survival of a small portion of their stock. But this has escaped you, because for many generations the survivors passed on without leaving a written record. Indeed, Solon, there was a time, before the greatest of these devastating floods, when the city that is Athens today not only excelled in war but also distinguished itself by the excellence of its laws in every area. Its accomplishments and its social arrangements are said to have been the finest of all those under heaven of which we have re- *d* ceived report.'

"When Solon heard this he was astounded, he said, and with unreserved eagerness begged the priests to give him a detailed, consecutive account of all that concerned those ancient citizens. 'I won't grudge you this, Solon,' the priest replied. 'I'll tell you the story for your own benefit as well as your city's, and especially in honor of our patron goddess who has founded, nurtured, and educated our cities, both yours and ours. Yours she founded first, a thousand years before ours, when she had received from Earth *e* and Hephaestus the seed from which your people were to come. Now our social arrangement, according to the records inscribed in our sacred documents, is eight thousand years old. Nine thousand years ago, then, did these fellow citizens of yours live, whose laws and whose finest achievement I'll briefly describe to you. At another time we'll go through all the details one by one at our 24 leisure and inspect the documents themselves.

" 'Let's compare your ancient laws with ours today. You'll discover many instances that once existed among you, existing among us today. First, you'll find that the class of priests is marked off and separated from the other classes. Next, in the case of the working class, you'll find that each group—the herdsmen, the hunters, and the farmers—works independently, without mixing with the others. In particular, I'm sure you've noticed that our *b* warrior class has been separated from all the others. It's been assigned by law to occupy itself exclusively with matters of war.

Moreover, the style of armor used is that of shields and spears, which we were the first among the peoples of Asia to use for arming ourselves. The goddess instructed us just as she first instructed you in the regions where you live. Furthermore, as for wisdom, I'm sure you can see how much attention our way of
c life here has devoted to it, right from the beginning. In our study of the world order we have traced all our discoveries, including prophecy and health-restoring medicine, from those divine realities to human levels, and we have also acquired all the other related disciplines. This is in fact nothing less than the very same system of social order that the goddess first devised for you when she founded your city, which she did once she had chosen the region in which your people were born and had discerned that the temperate climate in it throughout the seasons would bring
d forth men of surpassing wisdom. And, being a lover of both war and wisdom, the goddess chose the region that was likely to bring forth men most like herself, and founded it first. And so you came to live there, and to observe laws such as these. Indeed your laws improved even more, so that you came to surpass all other peoples in every excellence, as could be expected from those whose begetting and nurture were divine.

" 'Now many great accomplishments of your city recorded
e here are awe-inspiring, but there is one that surely surpasses them all in magnitude and excellence. The records speak of a vast power that your city once brought to a halt in its insolent march against the whole of Europe and Asia at once—a power that sprang forth from beyond, from the Atlantic Ocean. For at that time this ocean was passable, since it had an island in it in front of the strait that you people say you call the Pillars of Heracles.[9] This island was larger than Libya and Asia combined, and it provided passage to the other islands for people who traveled in those days. From
25 those islands one could then travel to the entire continent on the other side, which surrounds that real sea beyond. Everything here inside the strait we're talking about seems nothing but a harbor with a narrow entrance, whereas that really is an ocean out there and the land that embraces it all the way around truly deserves to be called a continent. Now on this Isle of Atlantis a great and marvelous royal power established itself and ruled not only the whole island, but many of the other islands and parts of the continent as well. What's more, its rule extended even inside

---

9. The Strait of Gibraltar.

the strait, over Libya as far as Egypt and over Europe as far as   *b*
Tyrrhenia.[10] Now one day this power gathered all of itself together
and set out to enslave all the territory inside the strait, including
your region and ours, in one fell swoop. Then it was, Solon, that
your city's might shone bright with excellence and strength for
all humankind to see. Preeminent among all others in the nobility
of her spirit and in her use of all the arts of war, she first rose to   *c*
the leadership of the Greek cause. Later, forced to stand alone,
deserted by her allies, she reached a point of extreme peril. Nevertheless she overcame the invaders and erected her monument of
victory. She prevented the enslavement of those not yet enslaved
and generously freed all the rest of us who lived within the
boundaries of Heracles. Sometime later, excessively violent earth-
quakes and floods occurred, and after the onset of an unbearable   *d*
day and a night, your entire warrior force sank below the earth
all at once, and the Isle of Atlantis likewise sank below the sea
and disappeared. That is how the ocean in that region has come
to be even now unnavigable and unexplorable, obstructed as it
is by a layer of mud at a shallow depth,[11] the residue of the island
as it settled.' "

What I've just related, Socrates, is a concise version of old   *e*
Critias' story, as Solon originally reported it. While you were
speaking yesterday about politics and the men you were describing, I was reminded of what I've just told you and was quite
amazed as I realized how by some supernatural chance your ideas
are on the mark, in substantial agreement with what Solon said.
I didn't want to say so at the time, though. It was so long ago, I   *26*
didn't remember Solon's story very well. So I realized that I would
first have to recover the whole story for myself well enough, and
then to tell it that way. That's why I was so quick to agree to
your assignment yesterday. The most important task in situations
like these is to propose a speech that rewards people's expecta-
tions, and so I thought we would be well supplied if I gave
this one. And that's how—as Hermocrates has already said—the
moment I left here yesterday, I began to repeat the story to him   *b*
and to Timaeus as it came back to me. After I left them, I concen-
trated on it during the night and recovered just about the whole
thing. They say that the lessons of childhood have a marvelous

---

10. South of the Mediterranean the empire extended across North Africa to the
western frontier of Egypt. To the north it included Europe as far east as central Italy.

11. Reading *kata bracheos*. Compare Cornford [14], pp. 366–67.

way of being retained. How true that is! In my case, I don't know if I'd be able to recall everything I heard yesterday, but I'd be extremely surprised if any part of this story has gotten away from me, even though it's been a very long time since I heard it. What

c I heard then gave me so much childlike pleasure—the old man was so eager to teach me because I kept on asking one question after another—that the story has stayed with me like the indelible markings of a picture with the colors burnt in. Besides, I told the whole story to Timaeus and Hermocrates first thing this morning, so that not just I, but they, too, would have a supply of material for our speech.

I've said all this, Socrates, to prepare myself to tell Solon's story now. I won't just give you the main points, but the details, one by one, just the way I heard it. We'll translate the citizens and the city you described to us in mythical fashion yesterday

d to the realm of fact, and place it before us as though it were ancient Athens itself. And we'll say that the citizens you imagined are the very ones the priest spoke about, our actual ancestors. The congruence will be complete, and our song will be in tune if we say that your imaginary citizens are the ones who really existed at that time. We'll share the task among us, and we'll all try our best to do justice to your assignment. What do you think,

e Socrates? Will this do as our speech, or should we look for another to replace it?

SOCRATES: Well, Critias, what other speech could we possibly prefer to this one? We're in the midst of celebrating the festival of the goddess, and this speech really fits the occasion. So it couldn't be more appropriate. And of course the fact that it's no made-up story, but a true account, is no small matter. How and where shall we find others to celebrate if we let these men go? We've no choice. Go on with your speech, then, and good luck!

27 It's my turn now to sit back and listen to your speeches that pay back mine of yesterday.

CRITIAS: All right, Socrates, what do you think of the plan we've arranged for our guest gift to you? We thought that because Timaeus is our expert in astronomy and has made it his main business to know the nature of the universe, he should speak first, beginning with the origin of the world and concluding with the nature of human beings. Then I'll go next, once I'm in posses-

sion of Timaeus' account of the origin of human beings and your
account of how some of them came to have a superior education. *b*
I'll introduce them, as not only Solon's account but also his law
would have it, into our courtroom and make them citizens of our
ancient city—as really being those Athenians of old whom the
report of the sacred records has rescued from obscurity—and
from then on I'll speak of them as actual Athenian citizens.

SOCRATES: Apparently I'll be getting a complete, brilliant ban-
quet of speeches in payment for my own. Very well then, Timaeus,
the task of being our next speaker seems to fall to you. Why don't
you make an invocation to the gods, as we customarily do?

TIMAEUS: That I will, Socrates. Surely anyone with any sense *c*
at all will always call upon a god before setting out on any venture,
whatever its importance. In our case, we are about to make
speeches about the universe—whether it has an origin or even if
it does not[12]—and so if we're not to go completely astray we have
no choice but to call upon the gods and goddesses, and pray that
they above all will approve of all we have to say, and that in
consequence we will, too. Let this, then, be our appeal to the *d*
gods; to ourselves we must appeal to make sure that you learn
as easily as possible, and that I instruct you in the subject matter
before us in the way that best conveys my intent.

As I see it, then, we must begin by making the following
distinction: What is *that which always is* and has no becoming, and
what is *that which becomes*[13] but never is? The former is grasped *28*
by understanding, which involves a reasoned account. It is unchanging. The latter is grasped by opinion, which involves unreasoning sense perception. It comes to be and passes away but
never really is. Now everything that comes to be[14] must of necessity come to be by the agency of some cause, for it is impossible
for anything to come to be without a cause. So whenever the

---

12. Reading *ei gegonen ē kai agenes estin*. See Whittaker [102], also Dillon [54],
pp. 57–60.

13. Omitting *aei*, which is poorly attested. See Whittaker [102] and [103], also
Dillon [54], pp. 60–63.

14. *Becoming* and *coming to be* here as elsewhere translate the same Greek word,
genesis and its cognates. The Greek word does not say, as English "comes to be"
does, that once a thing has come to be, it now *is*, or has *being*.

craftsman[15] looks at what is always changeless and, using a thing
of that kind as his model, reproduces its form and character, then,
b of necessity, all that he so completes is beautiful. But were he to
look at a thing that has come to be and use as his model something
that has been begotten, his work will lack beauty.

Now as to the whole heaven [*ouranos*], or world order [*kosmos*]—let's just call it by whatever name is most acceptable in a
given context[16]—there is a question we need to consider first. This
is the sort of question one should begin with in inquiring into
any subject. Has it always been? Was there no origin [*archē*] from
which it came to be? Or did it come to be and take its start from
some origin? It has come to be. For it is both visible and tangible
and it has a body—and all things of that kind are perceptible.
c And, as we have shown, perceptible things are grasped by opinion, which involves sense perception. As such, they are things
that come to be, things that are begotten. Further, we maintain
that, necessarily, that which comes to be must come to be by the
agency of some cause. Now to find the maker and father of this
universe [*to pan*] is hard enough, and even if I succeeded, to
declare him to everyone is impossible. And so we must go back
and raise this question about the universe: Which of the two
29 models did the maker use when he fashioned it? Was it the one
that does not change and stays the same, or the one that has come
to be? Well, if this world of ours is beautiful and its craftsman
good, then clearly he looked at the eternal model. But if what it's
blasphemous to even say is the case, then he looked at one that
has come to be. Now surely it's clear to all that it was the eternal
model he looked at, for, of all the things that have come to be,
our world is the most beautiful, and of causes the craftsman is
the most excellent. This, then, is how it has come to be: it is a work
of craft, modeled after that which is changeless and is grasped by
a rational account, that is, by wisdom.
b   Since these things are so, it follows by unquestionable neces-

---

15. Greek *dēmiourgos*, also sometimes translated below as "maker" (40c2, 41a7)
or "one who fashions" (69c3)—whence the divine "demiurge" one reads about
in accounts of the *Timaeus*.

16. The three primary terms Plato uses to refer to the universe are *ouranos*
("heaven" or "heavens"), *kosmos* ("world" or "world order"), and *to pan* ("universe"—lit. "the whole"). The first of these is properly the designation for the
realm of the fixed stars (at, e.g., 37d6, e2, 38b6) but is also used to designate the
universe as a whole (at, e.g., 31a2, b3). The second refers to the world as an
orderly system, while the third considers it in its totality.

sity that this world is an image of something. Now in every subject it is of utmost importance to begin at the natural beginning, and so, on the subject of an image and its model, we must make the following specification: the accounts we give of things have the same character as the subjects they set forth. So accounts of what is stable and fixed and transparent to understanding are themselves stable and unshifting. We must do our very best to make these accounts as irrefutable and invincible as any account may be. On the other hand, accounts we give of that which has been formed to be like that reality, since they are accounts of what is a likeness, are themselves likely, and stand in proportion to the previous accounts, that is, what being is to becoming, truth is to convincingness. Don't be surprised then, Socrates, if it turns out repeatedly that we won't be able to produce accounts on a great many subjects—on gods or the coming to be of the universe—that are completely and perfectly consistent and accurate. Instead, if we can come up with accounts no less likely than any, we ought to be content, keeping in mind that both I, the speaker, and you, the judges, are only human. So we should accept the likely tale on these matters. It behooves us not to look for anything beyond this.

SOCRATES: Bravo, Timaeus! By all means! We must accept it as you say we should. This overture of yours was marvelous. Go on now and let us have the work itself.

TIMAEUS: Very well, then. Now why did he who framed this whole universe of becoming frame it? Let us state the reason why: He was good, and one who is good can never become jealous of anything. And so, being free of jealousy, he wanted everything to become as much like himself as was possible. In fact, men of wisdom will tell you (and you couldn't do better than to accept their claim) that this, more than anything else, was the most preeminent reason for the origin of the world's coming to be. The god wanted everything to be good and nothing to be bad so far as that was possible, and so he took over all that was visible—not at rest but in discordant and disorderly motion[17]—and brought it from a state of disorder to one of order, because he believed that order was in every way better than disorder. Now it wasn't permitted (nor is it now) that one who is supremely good should do anything but what is best. Accordingly, the god reasoned

---

17. See below, 52e–53b.

and concluded that in the realm of things naturally visible no
unintelligent thing could as a whole be better than anything that
does possess intelligence as a whole, and he further concluded
that it is impossible for anything to come to possess intelligence
apart from soul. Guided by this reasoning, he put intelligence in
soul, and soul in body, and so he constructed the universe. He
wanted to produce a piece of work that would be as excellent
and supreme as its nature would allow. This, then, in keeping
with our likely account, is how we must say divine providence
c brought our world into being as a truly living thing, endowed
with soul and intelligence.

This being so, we have to go on to speak about what comes
next. When the maker made our world, what living thing did he
make it resemble? Let us not stoop to think that it was any of
those that have the natural character of a part,[18] for nothing that
is a likeness of anything incomplete could ever turn out beautiful.
Rather, let us lay it down that the world resembles more closely
than anything else that Living Thing of which all other living
things are parts, both individually and by kinds. For that Living
Thing comprehends within itself all intelligible living things, just
d as our world is made up of us and all the other visible creatures.
Since the god wanted nothing more than to make the world like
the best of the intelligible things, complete in every way, he made
31 it a single visible living thing, which contains within itself all the
living things whose nature it is to share its kind.

Have we been correct in speaking of *one* heaven, or would it
have been more correct to say that there are many, in fact infinitely
many? There is but one, if it is to have been crafted after its model.
For that which contains all of the intelligible living things couldn't
ever be one of a pair, since that would require there to be yet
another Living Thing, the one that contained those two, of which
they then would be parts,[19] and then it would be more correct to
speak of our heaven as made in the likeness, now not of those
b two, but of that other, the one that contains them. So, in order
that this living thing should be like the complete Living Thing
in respect of uniqueness, the maker made neither two, nor yet
an infinite number of worlds. On the contrary, our heaven came
to be as the one and only thing of its kind, is so now, and will
continue to be so in the future.

Now that which comes to be must have bodily form, and be

---

18. Greek *morion*, which often in Plato refers to species.

19. See previous note.

both visible and tangible, but nothing could ever become visible apart from fire, nor tangible without something solid, nor solid without earth. That is why, as he began to put the body of the universe together, the god came to make it out of fire and earth. But it isn't possible to combine two things well all by themselves, without a third; there has to be some bond between the two that *c* unites them. Now the best bond is one that really and truly makes a unity of itself together with the things bonded by it, and this in the nature of things is best accomplished by proportion. For whenever of three numbers (or bulks or powers)[20] the middle 32 term between any two of them is such that what the first term is to it, it is to the last, and, conversely, what the last term is to the middle, it is to the first, then, since the middle term turns out to be both first and last, and the last and the first likewise both turn out to be middle terms, they will all of necessity turn out to have the same relationship to each other, and, given this, will all be unified.

So if the body of the universe were to have come to be as a two-dimensional plane, a single middle term would have sufficed *b* to bind together its conjoining terms with itself. As it was, however, the universe was to be a solid, and solids are never joined together by just one middle term but always by two. Hence the god set water and air between fire and earth, and made them as proportionate to one another as was possible, so that what fire is to air, air is to water, and what air is to water, water is to earth. He then bound them together and thus he constructed the visible and tangible heavens. This is the reason why these four particular *c* constituents were used to beget the body of the world, making it a symphony of proportion.[21] They bestowed friendship[22] upon it, so that, having come together into a unity with itself, it could not be undone by anyone but the one who had bound it together.

Now each one of the four constituents was entirely used up

---

20. Following Pritchard [88].

21. A simple example of a proportionate progression of numbers that satisfies Plato's requirements in 32a might be that of 2, 4, 8. So: 2:4::4:8 (the first term is to the middle what the middle is to the last, the last term is to the middle what the middle is to the first); 4:2::8:4 or 4:8::2:4 (the middle term turns out to be first and last and the first and last terms turn out to be middles). Since, however, the body of the world is three-dimensional, its components must be represented by a geometrical progression that will require two middle terms.

22. Compare *Gorgias* 508a: "Wise men claim that partnership and friendship . . . hold together heaven and earth . . . and that is why they call this universe a *world-order. . . .*"

in the process of building the world. The builder built it from all
the fire, water, air, and earth there was, and left no part or power
d of any of them out. His intentions in so doing were these: First,
that as a living thing it should be as whole and complete as
33 possible and made up of complete parts. Second, that it should
be just one world, in that nothing would be left over from which
another one just like it could be made. Third, that it should not
get old and diseased. He realized that when hot or cold things or
anything else that possesses strong powers surrounds a composite
body from outside and attacks it, it destroys that body prema-
turely, brings disease and old age upon it and so causes it to
waste away. That is why he concluded that he should fashion
the world as a single whole, composed of all wholes, complete
and free of old age and disease, and why he fashioned it that
b way. And he gave it a shape appropriate to the kind of thing it
was. The appropriate shape for that living thing that is to contain
within itself all the living things would be the one which embraces
within itself all the shapes there are. Hence he gave it a round
shape, the form of a sphere, with its center equidistant from its
extremes in all directions. This of all shapes is the most complete
and most like itself, which he gave to it because he believed that
likeness is incalculably more excellent than unlikeness. And he
c gave it a smooth, round finish all over on the outside, for many
reasons. It needed no eyes, since there was nothing visible left
outside it; nor did it need ears, since there was nothing audible
there, either. There was no air enveloping it that it might need
for breathing, nor did it need any organ by which to take in food
or, again, expel it when it had been digested. For since there
wasn't anything else, there would be nothing to leave it or come
to it from anywhere. It supplied its own waste for its food. Anything that it did or experienced it was designed to do or experience
d within itself and by itself. For the builder thought that if it were
self-sufficient, it would be a better thing than if it required
other things.

And since it had no need to catch hold of or fend off anything,
the god thought that it would be pointless to attach hands to it.
34 Nor would it need feet or any support to stand on. In fact, he
awarded it the movement suited to its body—that one of the
seven motions which is especially associated with understanding
and intelligence. And so he set it turning continuously in the
same place, spinning around upon itself. All the other six motions
he took away, and made its movement free of their wanderings.

And since it didn't need feet to follow this circular path, he begat it without legs or feet.

Applying this entire train of reasoning to the god that was *b*
yet to be, the eternal god made it smooth and even all over, equal from the center, a whole and complete body itself, but also made up of complete bodies. In its center he set a soul, which he extended throughout the whole body and with which he then covered the body outside. And he set it to turn in a circle, a single solitary heaven, whose very excellence enables it to keep its own company without requiring anything else. For its knowledge of and friendship with itself is enough. All this, then, explains why this world which he begat for himself is a blessed god.

As for the world's soul, even though we are now embarking on an account of it *after* we've already given an account of its body, it isn't the case that the god devised it to be younger than *c*
the body. For the god would not have united them and then allow the elder to be ruled by the younger. We have a tendency to be casual and random in our speech, reflecting, no doubt, the whole realm of the casual and random of which we are a part. The god, however, gave priority and seniority to the soul, both in its coming to be and in the degree of its excellence, to be the body's mistress and to rule over it as her subject.

The components from which he made the soul and the way 35
in which he made it were as follows: In between the *Being* that is indivisible and always changeless, and the one that is divisible and comes to be in the corporeal realm, he mixed a third, intermediate form of being, derived from the other two. Similarly, he made a mixture of *the Same*, and then one of *the Different*, in between their indivisible and their corporeal, divisible counterparts.[23] And he took the three mixtures and mixed them together to make a uniform mixture, forcing the Different, which was hard to mix, into conformity with the Same. Now when he had mixed *b*
these two together with Being, and from the three had made a single mixture, he redivided the whole mixture into as many parts as his task required,[24] each part remaining a mixture of the Same, the Different, and of Being. This is how he began the division:

---

23. The translation follows the construction given by Proclus. For a defense, see Grube [61].

24. In order to establish in the soul, through connected geometrical proportions, the source of the harmonious order it needs to impart to the three-dimensional body of the world, and in particular to the heaven and the bodies it contains.

First he took one portion away from the whole, and then he took another, twice as large, followed by a third, one and a half times as large as the second and three times as large as the first. The fourth portion he took was twice as large as the second, the fifth three times as large as the third, the sixth eight times that of the first, and the seventh twenty-seven times that of the first.

36   After this he went on to fill the double and triple intervals by cutting off still more portions from the mixture and placing these between them, in such a way that in each interval there were two middle terms, one exceeding the first extreme by the same fraction of the extremes by which it was exceeded by the second, and the other exceeding the first extreme by a number equal to that by which it was exceeded by the second. These connections produced intervals of ³⁄₂, ⁴⁄₃, and ⁹⁄₈ within the previous intervals. He then
b   proceeded to fill all the ⁴⁄₃ intervals with the ⁹⁄₈ interval, leaving a small portion over every time. The terms of this interval of the portion left over made a numerical ratio of ²⁵⁶⁄₂₄₃. And so it was that the mixture, from which he had cut off these portions, was eventually completely used up.²⁵

---

25. The construction of the world's soul follows three stages:

1. *The creation of the mixture:* Three preliminary mixtures are created. The first is a mixture of indivisible, changeless Being with divisible Being. The second and third are likewise mixtures of indivisible with divisible Sameness and Difference, respectively. These three preliminary mixtures are themselves mixed to create the final mixture.

2. *The division of the mixture:* Seven "portions" of the mixture are now marked off, possessing the following numerical values:

First portion:	1	Fifth portion:	9
Second portion:	2	Sixth portion:	8
Third portion:	3	Seventh portion:	27
Fourth portion:	4		

3. *The filling of the intervals:* The values of the first, second, fourth, and sixth portions form a series such that each successive portion is twice that of its predecessor. The values of the first, third, fifth, and seventh portions form a series such that each successive portion is three times that of its predecessor. Thus intervals between successive portions of the first series are called "double intervals," and those between successive portions of the second series are called "triple intervals." Within each interval there are two "middle terms." The first of these is such that its value is that of the first extreme plus $1/x$ of the first extreme, which is equal to the value of the second extreme minus $1/x$ of the second extreme. This is the "harmonic middle." The second middle term is such that its value is the median between the extremes. This is the "arithmetical middle."

Next, he sliced this entire compound in two along its length, joined the two halves together center to center like an X, and bent c
them back in a circle, attaching each half to itself end to end and to the ends of the other half at the point opposite to the one where they had been joined together. He then included them in that motion which revolves in the same place without variation, and began to make the one the outer, and the other the inner, circle. And he decreed that the outer movement should be the movement of *the Same,* while the inner one should be that of *the Different.* He made the movement of the Same revolve toward the right by way of the side, and that of the Different toward the left by way of the diagonal, and he made the revolution of the Same, that is, d
the uniform, the dominant one in that he left this one alone undivided, while he divided the inner one six times, to make seven unequal circles. His divisions corresponded to the several double and triple intervals, of which there were three each.[26] He

---

Inserting the two middle terms within the original intervals in the first series, we get:

1—$4/3$—$3/2$—**2**—$8/3$—3—**4**—$16/3$—6—**8**; and doing the same with the second series produces:

1—$3/2$—2—**3**—$9/2$—6—**9**—$27/2$—18—**27**.

Combining the two series in ascending order and omitting duplication we get:

1—$4/3$—$3/2$—**2**—$8/3$—**3**—**4**—$9/2$—$16/3$—6—**8**—**9**—$27/2$—18—**27**.

In this series the value of each term but the first is either $4/3$ or $3/2$ or $9/8$ the value of its predecessor. Finally, the intervals of $4/3$ (e.g., between 1 and $4/3$, or between $3/2$ and 2, or 3 and 4) are now themselves "filled" by intervals of $9/8$. In the interval between 1 and $4/3$, for example, we can insert new intervals, each of which multiplies its predecessor by $9/8$, but we can do so no more than twice (**1**—$9/8$—$81/64$ . . . . $4/3$), since a third attempt ($729/512$) would exceed $4/3$. The interval between $81/64$ can only be filled up with a "leftover," a number by which $81/64$ can be multiplied to equal $4/3$. This number turns out to be $256/243$.

4. *The creation of the circles of the Same and the Different:* The stuff thus arranged is cut lengthwise into two strips that are fastened center to center, and the ends of each connected together. The outer strip is the circle of the Same, and the inner one that of the Different. For the positions and movements of these circles, see the next note.

26. By speaking of "circles" instead of spheres, Plato seems to have in mind the model of an armillary sphere (so Cornford [14], pp. 74–77, though this is sharply disputed by Dicks [17], pp. 120–21), a skeleton structure that, by representing whole spheres as bands, enables a viewer to examine the axial positions of spheres within the outer sphere. The outer band is the circle responsible for the constant

set the circles to go in contrary directions[27]: three to go at the same speed, and the other four to go at speeds different from both each other's and that of the other three. Their movements, however, were all proportionate to each other.[28]

Once the whole soul had acquired a form that pleased him,
e he who formed it went on to fashion inside it all that is corporeal, and, joining center to center, he fitted the two together. The soul

---

daily rotation of the fixed stars—hence for the "movement of *the Same*." That movement pervades the entire sphere, from the center of the earth to the universe's outer limit, the realm of the fixed stars. This sphere moves "toward the right," that is, from east to west along its axis between the poles (NS) along the plane of the equator (CD). The observation point is presumably that of an observer in a northern latitude looking toward the south (Vlastos [41], p. 34, n. 23, but see *contra* Dicks [17], p. 122). The circle of *the Different* is a band that is subsequently subdivided into seven smaller bands (spheres), the orbits of the seven "wandering" stars—the moon, the sun, and the five planets known to the ancients, Mercury, Venus, Mars, Jupiter, and Saturn. It is responsible for imparting to them a motion "toward the left," that is, roughly from west to east (allowing for the angle of inclination), the opposite direction from that of the movement of *the Same*, the sphere that embraces them. The planes of these seven bands are not necessarily parallel to "the diagonal" (see Introduction, n. 88), that is, the plane of the ecliptic (EB) circumscribed by the Zodiac, that band of constellations which parallels, and is bisected along its length by, the ecliptic. The relation of the plane of the equator to that of the ecliptic, following Plato's suggestion that the latter is "diagonal" to the former, is illustrated below. Compare also the illustrations in Dicks [17], p. 122, and Vlastos [41], p. 56.

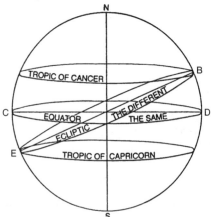

27. For a brief discussion of the difficulties raised by this description, see the Introduction, pp. xlv–xlvi.

28. The sun, Venus, and Mercury are the three described as going "at the same speed." Compare 38d below.

was woven together with the body from the center on out in every direction to the outermost limit of the heavens, and covered it all around on the outside. And, revolving within itself, it initiated a divine beginning of unceasing, intelligent life for all time. Now while the body of the heavens had come to be as a visible thing, the soul was invisible. But even so, because it shares in reason and harmony, the soul came to be as the most excellent 37 of all the things begotten by him who is himself most excellent of all that is intelligible and eternal.

Because the soul is a mixture of the Same, the Different, and Being (the three components we've described), because it was divided up and bound together in various proportions, and because it circles round upon itself, then, whenever it comes into contact with something whose being is scatterable or else with something whose being is indivisible, it is stirred throughout its whole self. It then declares what exactly that thing is the same as, or what it is different from, and in what respect and in what b manner, as well as when, it turns out that they are the same or different and are characterized as such.[29] This applies both to the things that come to be, and to those that are always changeless. And when this contact gives rise to an account that is equally true whether it is about what is different or about what is the same, and is borne along without utterance or sound within the self-moved thing, then, whenever the account concerns anything that is perceptible, the circle of the Different goes straight and proclaims it throughout its whole soul. This is how firm and true opinions and convictions come about. Whenever, on the other c hand, the account concerns any object of reasoning, and the circle of the Same runs well and reveals it, the necessary result is understanding and knowledge. And if anyone should ever call that in which these two arise not soul, but something else, what he says will be anything but true.

Now when the father who had begotten the universe observed it set in motion and alive, a thing that had come to be as a shrine for the everlasting gods, he was well pleased, and in his delight he thought of making it more like its model still. So, as the model d

---

29. Plato relies on a principle, common to some fifth-century natural philosophers (e.g., Empedocles), that "like is known by like": in order for a knowing subject to be able to know a given object, the subject must possess some of the same or similar characteristics as the object. Thus because the soul is itself composed of sameness and difference, it can recognize A as being the same as or different from B, and the respects, manners, and times when this is so.

was itself an everlasting Living Thing, he set himself to bringing this universe to completion in such a way that it, too, would have that character to the extent that it was possible. Now it was the Living Thing's nature to be eternal, but it isn't possible to bestow eternity fully upon anything that is begotten. And so he began to think of making a moving image of eternity: at the same time as he brought order to the heavens, he would make an eternal image, moving according to number, of eternity remaining in unity. This image, of course, is what we now call "time."

e   For before the heavens came to be, there were no days or nights, no months or years. But now, at the same time as he framed the heavens, he devised their coming to be. These all are parts of time, and *was* and *will be* are forms of time that have come to be. Such notions we unthinkingly but incorrectly apply to everlasting being. For we say that it *was* and *is* and *will be*, but

38   according to the true account only *is* is appropriately said of it. *Was* and *will be* are properly said about the becoming that passes in time, for these two are motions. But that which is always changeless and motionless cannot become either older or younger in the course of time—it neither ever became so, nor is it now such that it has become so, nor will it ever be so in the future. And all in all, none of the characteristics that becoming has bestowed upon the things that are borne about in the realm of perception are appropriate to it. These, rather, are forms of time that have come to be—time that imitates eternity and circles according to number. And what is more, we also say things like

b   these: that what has come to be *is* what has come to be, that what is coming to be *is* what is coming to be, and also that what will come to be *is* what will come to be, and that what is not *is* what is not. None of these expressions of ours is accurate. But I don't suppose this is a good time right now to be too meticulous about these matters.

Time, then, came to be together with the heavens so that just as they were begotten together, they might also be undone together, should there ever be an undoing of them. And it came to be after the model of that which is sempiternal,[30] so that it

c   might be as much like its model as possible. For the model is something that has being *for all eternity*, while it, on the other hand, has been, is, and shall be *for all time*, forevermore. Such was the reason, then, such the god's design for the coming to be

---

30. Greek *diaiōnia*—also at 39e2—an exotic word, possibly Plato's own invention.

of time, that he brought into being the Sun, the Moon, and five other stars, for the begetting of time. These are called "wanderers" [*planēta*], and they came to be in order to set limits to and stand guard over the numbers of time. When the god had finished making a body for each of them, he placed them into the orbits traced by the period of the Different—seven bodies in seven orbits. *d* He set the Moon in the first circle, around the earth, and the Sun in the second, above it. The Dawnbearer [the Morning Star, or Venus] and the star said to be sacred to Hermes [Mercury] he set to run in circles that equal the Sun's in speed, though they received the power contrary to its power. As a result, the Sun, the star of Hermes, and the Dawnbearer alike overtake and are overtaken by one another. As for the other bodies, if I were to spell out where he situated them, and all his reasons for doing so, my account, already a digression, would make more work than its *e* purpose calls for. Perhaps later on we could at our leisure give this subject the exposition it deserves.

Now when each of the bodies that were to cooperate in producing time had come into the movement prepared for carrying it and when, bound by bonds of soul, these bodies had been begotten with life and learned their assigned tasks, they began to revolve along the movement of the Different, which is oblique and *39* which goes through the movement of the Same, by which it is also dominated.[31] Some bodies would move in a larger circle, others in a smaller one, the latter moving more quickly and the former more slowly. Indeed, because of the movement of the Same, the ones that go around most quickly appeared to be overtaken by those going more slowly, even though in fact they were overtaking them. For as it revolves, this movement gives to all these circles a spiral twist, because they are moving forward in *b* two contrary directions at once.[32] As a result, it makes that body which departs most slowly from it—and it is the fastest of the movements—appear closest to it.

And so that there might be a conspicuous measure of their relative slowness and quickness with which[33] they move along in their eight revolutions, the god kindled a light in the orbit second from the earth, the light that we now call the Sun. Its chief work would be to shine upon the whole heaven and to bestow

---

31. Reading *iousēn . . . kratoumenēn*. The description refers back to 36c–d.

32. Compare 36d4–5.

33. Accepting the emendation *kath' ha* (with Archer-Hind [4], pp. 128–29).

upon all those living things appropriately endowed and taught
by the revolution of the Same and the uniform, a share in number.
c In this way and for these reasons night-and-day, the period of a
single circling, the wisest one, came to be. A month has passed
when the Moon has completed its own cycle and overtaken the
Sun; a year when the Sun has completed its own cycle.

As for the periods of the other bodies [the five planets], all
but a scattered few have failed to take any note of them. Nobody
has given them names or investigated their numerical measure-
d ments relative to each other. And so people are all but ignorant
of the fact that time really is the wanderings of these bodies,
bewilderingly numerous as they are and astonishingly variegated.
It is nonetheless possible to discern that the perfect number of
time brings to completion the Perfect Year at that moment when
the relative speeds of all eight periods have been completed together and, measured by the circle of the Same that moves uniformly, have achieved their consummation. This, then, is how as
well as why those stars were begotten which, on their way through
the heavens, would have turnings. The purpose was to make this
e living thing as like as possible to that perfect and intelligible
Living Thing, by way of imitating its sempiternity.

Before the coming to be of time, the universe had already been
made to resemble in various respects the model in whose likeness
the god was making it, but the resemblance still fell short in that
it didn't yet contain all the living things that were to have come
to be within it. This remaining task he went on to perform, casting
the world into the nature of its model. And so he determined
that the Living Thing he was making should possess the same
kinds and numbers of living things as those which, according to
the discernment of Intellect, are contained within the real Living
Thing. Now there are four of these kinds: first, the heavenly race
40 of gods; next, the kind that has wings and travels through the
air; third, the kind that lives in water; and fourth, the kind that
has feet and lives on land. The gods he made mostly out of fire,
to be the brightest and fairest to the eye.[34] He made them well
rounded, to resemble the universe, and placed them in the wisdom of the dominant circle [i.e., of the Same], to follow the course
of the universe. He spread the gods throughout the whole heaven
to be a true adornment [*kosmos*] for it, an intricately wrought

---

34. These are the fixed stars, that is, those other than the planets, which have
already been created (cf. below, 40b).

whole. And he bestowed two movements upon each of them. The first was rotation, an unvarying movement in the same place, by which the god would always think the same thoughts about b the same things. The other was revolution, a forward motion under the dominance of the circular carrying movement of the Same and uniform. With respect to the other five motions the gods are immobile and stationary, in order that each of them may come as close as possible to attaining perfection.

This, then, was the reason why all those everlasting and un- wandering stars—divine living things that stay fixed by revolving without variation in the same place—came to be. Those that have turnings and thus wander in that sort of way came to be as previously described.

Earth he devised to be our nurturer, and, because it is packed around the axis[35] that stretches throughout the universe, also to c be the maker and guardian of day and night. Of the gods that have come to be within the heavens, Earth ranks as the foremost, the one with greatest seniority.

To describe the dancing movements of these gods, their juxta- positions and the back-circlings and advances of their circular courses on themselves; to tell which of the gods come into line with one another at their conjunctions and how many of them are in opposition, and in what order and at which times they pass in front of or behind one another, so that some are occluded from our view to reappear once again, thereby bringing terrors and portents of things to come to those who cannot reason—to d tell all this without the use of visible models would be labor spent in vain. We will make do with this account, and so let this be the conclusion of our discussion of the nature of the visible and generated gods.

As for the other spiritual beings [daimones], it is beyond our task to know and speak of how they came to be. We should accept on faith the assertions of those figures of the past who claimed to be the offspring of gods. They must surely have been well informed about their own ancestors. So we cannot avoid believing e the children of gods, even though their accounts lack plausible or compelling proofs. Rather, we should follow custom and believe them, on the ground that what they claim to be reporting are

---

35. Reading *eillomenēn*, though *illomenēn* ("winds around") cannot be ruled out. See Dicks [17], pp. 132–33 and p. 239, n. 181. For a discussion of whether this passage implies the axial rotation of the earth, see the Introduction, pp. xlix–l.

matters of their own concern. Accordingly, let us accept their account of how these gods came to be and state what it is.

Earth and Heaven gave birth to Ocean and Tethys, who in turn gave birth to Phorkys, Cronus, and Rhea and all the gods 41 in that generation. Cronus and Rhea gave birth to Zeus and Hera, as well as all those siblings who are called by names we know. These in turn gave birth to yet another generation. In any case, when all the gods had come to be, both the ones who make their rounds conspicuously and the ones who present themselves only to the extent that they are willing, the begetter of this universe spoke to them. This is what he said:

"O gods, works divine whose maker and father I am, whatever has come to be by my hands cannot be undone but by my con- b sent.[36] Now while it is true that anything that is bound is liable to being undone, still, only one who is evil would consent to the undoing of what has been well fitted together and is in fine condition. This is the reason why you, as creatures that have come to be, are neither completely immortal nor exempt from being undone. Still, you will not be undone nor will death be your portion, since you have received the guarantee of my will—a greater, more sovereign bond than those with which you were bound when you came to be. Learn now, therefore, what I declare to you. There remain still three kinds of mortal beings that have not yet been begotten; and as long as they have not come to be, the heaven will be incomplete, for it will still lack within it all c the kinds of living things it must have if it is to be sufficiently complete. But if these creatures came to be and came to share in life by my hand, they would rival the gods. It is you, then, who must turn yourselves to the task of fashioning these living things, as your nature allows. This will assure their mortality, and this whole universe will really be a completed whole. Imitate the power I used in causing you to be. And to the extent that it is fitting for them to possess something that shares our name of "immortal," something described as divine and ruling within those of them who always consent to follow after justice and after d you, I shall begin by sowing that seed, and then hand it over to you. The rest of the task is yours. Weave what is mortal to what is

---

36. Accepting the emendation *theiōn* and the supplement <*ta*> before *di' emou* in a7 (reading *theoi, theiōn hōn egō dēmiourgos patēr te ergōn, ta di' emou genomena aluta emou ge mē ethelontos*, following Robinson [90]).

immortal, fashion and beget living things. Give them food, cause them to grow, and when they perish, receive them back again."

When he had finished this speech, he turned again to the mixing bowl he had used before, the one in which he had blended and mixed the soul of the universe. He began to pour into it what remained of the previous ingredients[37] and to mix them in somewhat the same way, though these were no longer invariably and constantly pure, but of a second and third grade of purity. And when he had compounded it all, he divided the mixture into a number of souls equal to the number of the stars and assigned   *e* each soul to a star. He mounted each soul in a carriage, as it were, and showed it the nature of the universe. He described to them the laws that had been foreordained: They would all be assigned one and the same initial birth, so that none would be less well treated by him than any other. Then he would sow each of the souls into that instrument of time suitable to it, where they were to acquire the nature of being the most god-fearing of living   *42* things, and, since humans have a twofold nature, the superior kind should be such as would from then on be called "man."[38] So, once the souls were of necessity implanted in bodies, and these bodies had things coming to them and leaving them,[39] the first innate capacity they would of necessity come to have would be sense perception, which arises out of forceful disturbances.[40] This they all would have. The second would be love,[41] mingled with pleasure and pain. And they would come to have fear and spiritedness as well, plus whatever goes with having these emo-   *b* tions, as well as all their natural opposites. And if they could master these emotions, their lives would be just, whereas if they were mastered by them, they would be unjust. And if a person lived a good life throughout the due course of his time, he would at the end return to his dwelling place in his companion star, to live a life of happiness that agreed with his character. But if he

---

37. That is, portions of indivisible and divisible portions of Being, Sameness, and Difference. See above, 35a1 *ff.*

38. Greek *anēr*, male human being. Compare 90e–91a below and the Introduction, pp. lxxxviii–lxxxix.

39. Contrast the body of the universe, at 33c6–7 above.

40. See below, 61c–68d, esp. 64b, for the discussion of perceptual properties and the physiology of sense perception. For the discussion of pleasure and pain, see 64c–65b and 86b–87b.

41. Greek *erōs*.

c failed in this, he would be born a second time, now as a woman. And if even then he still could not refrain from wickedness, he would be changed once again, this time into some wild animal that resembled the wicked character he had acquired. And he would have no rest from these toilsome transformations until he had dragged that massive accretion of fire-water-air-earth into conformity with

d the revolution of the Same and uniform within him, and so subdued that turbulent, irrational mass by means of reason. This would return him to his original condition of excellence.

Having set out all these ordinances to them—which he did to exempt himself from responsibility for any evil they might afterward do—the god proceeded to sow some of them into the Earth, some into the Moon, and others into the various other instruments of time. After the sowing, he handed over to the young gods the task of weaving mortal bodies. He had them make whatever else remained that the human soul still needed

e to have, plus whatever goes with those things. He gave them the task of ruling over these mortal living things and of giving them the finest, the best possible guidance they could give, without being responsible for any evils these creatures might bring upon themselves.

When he had finished assigning all these tasks, he proceeded to abide at rest in his own customary nature. His children immediately began to attend to and obey their father's assignment. Now that they had received the immortal principle of the mortal living thing, they began to imitate the craftsman who had made them. They borrowed parts of fire, earth, water, and air from the world,

43 intending to pay them back again, and bonded together into a unity the parts they had taken, but not with those indissoluble bonds by which they themselves were held together. Instead, they proceeded to fuse them together with copious rivets so small as to be invisible, thereby making each body a unit made up of all the components. And they went on to invest this body—into and out of which things were to flow—with the orbits of the immortal soul. These orbits, now bound within a mighty river, neither mastered that river nor were mastered by it, but tossed it violently

b and were violently tossed by it. Consequently the living thing as a whole did indeed move, but it would proceed in a disorderly, random, and irrational way that involved all six of the motions.[42]

---

42. Timaeus is here describing the uncontrolled movements of a newborn infant. He goes on to describe the confusion produced in its soul by its first sensations.

It would go forward and backward, then back and forth to the right and the left, and upward and downward, wandering every which way in these six directions. For mighty as the nourishment-bearing billow was in its ebb and flow, mightier still was the turbulence produced by the disturbances caused by the things that struck against the living things. Such disturbances would occur when the body encountered and collided with external fire   c
(i.e., fire other than the body's own) or for that matter with a hard lump of earth or with the flow of gliding waters, or when it was caught up by a surge of air-driven winds. The motions produced by all these encounters would then be conducted through the body to the soul, and strike against it. (That is no doubt why these motions as a group came afterward to be called "sensations," as they are still called today.[43]) It was just then, at that very instant, that they produced a very long and intense commotion. They cooperated with the continually flowing chan-   d
nel to stir and violently shake the orbits of the soul. They completely bound that of the Same by flowing against it in the opposite direction, and held it fast just as it was beginning to go its way. And they further shook the orbit of the Different right through, with the result that they twisted every which way the three intervals of the double and the three of the triple, as well as the middle terms of the ratios of $3/2$, $4/3$, and $9/8$ that connect them.[44] [These agitations did not undo them, however,] because they cannot be completely undone except by the one who had bound them together. They mutilated and disfigured the circles in every possi-   e
ble way so that the circles barely held together and though they remained in motion, they moved without rhyme or reason, sometimes in the opposite direction, sometimes sideways and sometimes upside down—like a man upside down, head propped against the ground and holding his feet up against something. In that position his right side will present itself both to him and to those looking at him as left, and his left side as right. It is this very thing—and others like it—that had such a dramatic effect upon the revolutions of the soul. Whenever they encounter some-   44
thing outside of them characterizable as *same* or *different*, they will speak of it as "the same as" something, or as "different from"

---

43. It is not clear what etymological point involving the word *aesthēseis* (sensations) Plato wants to make here. He may think (incorrectly) that *aesthēsis* is etymologically related to *aïssein*, "to shake."

44. See 36b above and n. 25.

something else when the truth is just the opposite, so proving themselves to be misled and unintelligent. Also, at this stage souls do not have a ruling orbit taking the lead. And so when certain sensations come in from outside and attack them, they sweep the soul's entire vessel along with them. It is then that these revolutions, however much in control they seem to be, are actually under their control. All these disturbances are no doubt the reason why even today and not only at the beginning, whenever a soul
b   is bound within a mortal body, it at first lacks intelligence. But as the stream that brings growth and nourishment diminishes and the soul's orbits regain their composure, resume their proper courses, and establish themselves more and more with the passage of time, their revolutions are set straight, to conform to the configuration each of the circles takes in its natural course. They then correctly identify what is the same and what is different, and render intelligent the person who possesses them. And to be sure, if such a person also gets proper nurture to supplement his
c   education, he'll turn out perfectly whole and healthy, and will have escaped the most grievous of illnesses. But if he neglects this, he'll limp his way through life and return to Hades uninitiated and unintelligent.

But this doesn't happen until later. Our present subject, on the other hand, needs a more detailed treatment. We must move on to treat the prior questions—the ones that deal with how bodies came to be, part by part, as well as the soul. What were the gods' reasons, what was their plan when they caused these
d   to be? In discussing these questions, we shall hold fast to what is most likely, and proceed accordingly.

Copying the revolving shape of the universe, the gods bound the two divine orbits into a ball-shaped body, the part that we now call our head. This is the most divine part of us, and master of all our other parts. They then assembled the rest of the body and handed the whole of it to the head, to be in its service. They intended it to share in all the motions there were to be. To keep
e   the head from rolling around on the ground without any way of getting up over its various high spots and out of the low, they gave it the body as a vehicle to make its way easy. This is the reason why the body came to have length and grow four limbs that could flex and extend themselves, divinely devised for the purpose of getting about. Holding on and supporting itself with these limbs, it would be capable of making its way through all

regions, while carrying at the top the dwelling place of that most   45
divine, most sacred part of ourselves. This is how as well as why
we have all grown arms and legs. And considering the front side
to be more honorable and more commanding than the back, the
gods gave us the ability to travel for the most part in this direction.
Human beings no doubt ought to have the front sides of their
bodies distinguishable from and dissimilar to their backs, and so
the gods began by setting the face on that side of the head, the
soul's vessel. They bound organs inside it to provide completely   b
for the soul, and they assigned this side, the natural front, to be
the part that takes the lead.

The eyes were the first of the organs to be fashioned by the
gods, to conduct light. The reason why they fastened them within
the head is this. They contrived that such fire as was not for
burning but for providing a gentle light should become a body,
proper to each day. Now the pure fire inside us, cousin to that
fire, they made to flow through the eyes: so they made the eyes—
the eye as a whole but its middle in particular—close-textured,
smooth, and dense, to enable them to keep out all the other,   c
coarser stuff, and let that kind of fire pass through pure by itself.
Now whenever daylight surrounds the visual stream, like makes
contact with like and coalesces with it to make up a single homoge-
neous body aligned with the direction of the eyes. This happens
wherever the internal fire strikes and presses against an external
object it has connected with. And because this body of fire has
become uniform throughout and thus uniformly affected, it trans-
mits the motions of whatever it comes in contact with as well as   d
of whatever comes in contact with it, to and through the whole
body until they reach the soul. This brings about the sensation
we call "seeing." At night, however, the kindred fire has departed
and so the visual stream is cut off. For now it exits only to encounter something unlike itself. No longer able to bond with the surrounding air, which now has lost its fire, it undergoes changes
and dies out. So it not only stops seeing, but even begins to induce
sleep. For when the eyelids—which the gods devised to keep
eyesight safe—are closed, they shut in the power of the internal   e
fire, which then disperses and evens out the internal motions,
and when these have been evened out, a state of quietness ensues.
And if this quietness is deep, one falls into an all but dreamless
sleep. But if some fairly strong motions remain, they produce   46
images similar in kind and in number to the kinds of motions

they are, and the kinds of regions in which they remain—images which, though formed within, are recalled upon waking as external objects.

And so there is no longer any difficulty in understanding how images are produced in mirrors or in any other smooth reflecting surfaces. On such occasions the internal fire joins forces with the external fire, to form on the smooth surface a single fire that is *b* reshaped in a multitude of ways. So once the fire from the face comes to coalesce with the fire from sight on the smooth and bright surface, you have the inevitable appearance of all images of this sort. What is left will appear as right, because the parts of the fire from sight connect with the opposite parts of the fire from the face, contrary to the usual manner of encounter. But, on the other hand, what is right does appear as right, and what is left as left whenever light switches sides in the process of coalescing *c* with the light with which it coalesces. And this happens whenever the mirror's smooth surface is curled upwards on both sides, thereby bending the right part of the fire from sight toward the left, and the left part toward the right. And when this same smooth surface is turned along the length of the face [i.e., vertically], it makes the whole object appear upside down, because it bends the lower part of the ray toward the top and the upper part toward the bottom.[45]

Now all of the above are among the auxiliary causes employed in the service of the god as he does his utmost to bring to comple-

---

45. According to 45b–c, direct vision of an object in daylight occurs when fire exiting from the eyes coalesces with fire (daylight) traveling from the object to make a uniform, linear column of fire. In the case of seeing an object reflected in a mirror, the left side of the object will appear as its right side would appear if the object were directly seen, and vice versa, as the following diagram illustrates:

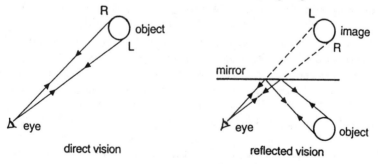

direct vision   reflected vision

tion the character of what is most excellent.[46] But because they *d*
make things cold or hot, compact or disperse them, and produce
all sorts of similar effects, most people regard them not as auxiliary
causes, but as the actual causes of all things. Things like these,
however, are totally incapable of possessing any reason or understanding about anything. We must pronounce the soul to be the
only thing there is that properly possesses understanding. The
soul is an invisible thing, whereas fire, water, earth, and air have
all come to be as visible bodies. So anyone who is a lover of
understanding and knowledge must of necessity pursue as primary causes those that belong to intelligent nature, and as second- *e*
ary all those belonging to things that are moved by others and
that set still others in motion by necessity. We too, surely, must
do likewise: we must describe both types of causes, distinguishing
those which possess understanding and thus fashion what is
beautiful and good, from those which, when deserted by intelligence, produce only haphazard and disorderly effects every time.

Let us conclude, then, our discussion of the accompanying
auxiliary causes that gave our eyes the power which they now
possess. We must next speak of that supremely beneficial function
for which the god gave them to us. As my account has it, our *47*
sight has indeed proved to be a source of supreme benefit to us,
in that none of our present statements about the universe could
ever have been made if we had never seen any stars, sun, or
heaven. As it is, however, our ability to see the periods of day-
and-night, of months and of years, of equinoxes and solstices,
has led to the invention of number and has given us the idea of
time and opened the path to inquiry into the nature of the universe. These pursuits have given us philosophy, a gift from the *b*
gods to the mortal race whose value neither has been nor ever
will be surpassed. I'm quite prepared to declare this to be the
supreme good our eyesight offers us. Why then should we exalt
all the lesser good things, which a nonphilosopher struck blind
would "lament and bewail in vain"[47]? Let us rather declare that
the cause and purpose of this supreme good is this: the god
invented sight and gave it to us so that we might observe the orbits
of intelligence in the heavens and apply them to the revolutions of

---

46. Greek: *tēn tou aristou . . . idean*. Plato may be referring to the Form of the
Good here.
47. A near-quotation from Euripides, *Phoenician Women*, l. 1762.

c our own understanding. For there is a kinship between them, even though our revolutions are disturbed, whereas the universal orbits are undisturbed. So once we have come to know them and to share in the ability to make correct calculations according to nature, we should stabilize the straying revolutions within ourselves by imitating the completely unstraying revolutions of the god.

Likewise, the same account goes for sound and hearing—these too are the gods' gifts, given for the same purpose and intended to achieve the same result. Speech (*logos*) was designed for this very purpose—it plays the greatest part in its achievement. And
d all such composition (*mousikē*) as lends itself to making audible musical sound (*phōnē*)[48] is given in order to express harmony, and so serves this purpose as well. And harmony, whose movements are akin to the orbits within our souls, is a gift of the Muses, if our dealings with them are guided by understanding, not for irrational pleasure, for which people nowadays seem to make use of it, but to serve as an ally in the fight to bring order to any orbit in our souls that has become unharmonized and make it concordant with itself. Rhythm, too, has likewise been given us
e by the Muses for the same purpose, to assist us. For with most of us our condition is such that we have lost all sense of measure, and are lacking in grace.

Now in all but a brief part of the discourse[49] I have just completed I have presented what has been crafted by Intellect (*nous*). But I need to match this account by providing a comparable one concerning the things that have come about by Necessity (*anankē*).
48 For this ordered world is of mixed birth: it is the offspring of a union of Necessity and Intellect. Intellect prevailed over Necessity by persuading it to direct most of the things that come to be toward what is best, and the result of this subjugation of Necessity to wise persuasion was the initial formation of this universe. So if I'm to tell the story of how it really came to be in this way, I'd also have to introduce the character of the Straying Cause—how
b it is its nature to set things adrift. I shall have to retrace my steps, then, and, armed with a second starting point that also applies to these same things, I must go back once again to the beginning and start my present inquiry from there, just as I did with my earlier one.

---

48. Reading *phōnēs*. See Cornford [14], p. 158, n. 4.
49. The exception was the discussion of the physiology of vision at 45b–46a.

We shall of course have to study the intrinsic nature of fire, water, air, and earth prior to the heaven's coming to be, as well as the properties [*pathē*] they had then. So far no one has revealed how these four came to be. We tend to posit them as the elemental "letters"[50] of the universe and tell people they are its "principles" [*archai*] on the assumption that they know what fire and the other three are. Actually, however, they shouldn't even be compared *c* to syllables.[51] Only a very unenlightened person might be expected to make such a comparison. So let me now proceed with my treatment in the following way: For the present I cannot state "the principle" or "principles" of all things, or however else I think about them, for the simple reason that it is difficult to show clearly what my view is if I follow my present manner of exposition. Please do not expect me to do so then. I couldn't convince even myself that I could be right to commit myself to *d* undertaking a task of such magnitude. I shall keep to what I stated at the beginning, the virtue of likely accounts, and so shall try right from the start to say about things, both individually and collectively, what is no less likely than any, more likely, in fact, than what I have said before.[52] Let us therefore at the outset of this discourse call upon the god to be our savior this time, too, to give us safe passage through a strange and unusual exposition, and lead us to a view of what is likely. And so let me begin my *e* speech again.

The new starting point in my account of the universe needs to be more complex than the earlier one. Then we distinguished two kinds, but now we must specify a third, one of a different sort. The earlier two sufficed for our previous account: one was proposed as a model, intelligible and always changeless, a second as an imitation of the model, something that possesses becoming *49* and is visible. We did not distinguish a third kind at the time, because we thought that we could make do with the two of them.

---

50. Greek *stoicheia*, which literally means "letters" but which in appropriate contexts can also be translated as "elements."

51. Plato is criticizing Empedocles and his followers, who made the familiar four elements the ultimate material constituents (the "roots") of things. As he argues later (53b–56c), the elements are composites made up of things that are themselves composite: the smallest "particle" of each element is a particular geometrical figure that is itself constituted by surfaces which in turn are composed of triangles. Each of these triangles is itself a complex of smaller triangles. See the Introduction, pp. lxvi–lxix.

52. Accepting the insertion of <*tōn*> after *mallon de*. See Taylor [39], pp. 310–11.

Now, however, it appears that our account compels us to attempt to illuminate in words a kind that is difficult and vague. What must we suppose it to do and to be? This above all: it is a *receptacle* of all becoming—its wetnurse, as it were.

However true that statement may be, we must nevertheless
b describe it more clearly. This is a difficult task, particularly because it requires us to raise a preliminary problem about fire and the other three: It is difficult to say of each of them—in a way that employs a reliable and stable account—which one is the sort of thing one should really call *water* rather than *fire*, or which one one should call some one of these rather than just any and every one of them. What problem, then, do they present for us to work through in likely fashion? And then how and in what manner are we to go on to speak about this third kind?[53]

First, we see (or think we see[54]) the thing that we have just now been calling *water* condensing and turning to stones and
c earth. Next, we see this same thing dissolving and dispersing, turning to wind and air, and air, when ignited, turning to fire. And then we see fire being condensed and extinguished and turning back to the form of air, and air coalescing and thickening and turning back into cloud and mist. When these are compressed still more we see them turning into flowing water, which we see turning to earth and stones once again. In this way, then, they transmit their coming to be one to the other in a cycle, or so it
d seems. Now then, since none of these appears ever to remain the same, which one of them can one categorically assert, without embarrassment, to be some particular thing, *this* one, and not something else? One can't. Rather, the safest course by far is to propose that we speak about these things in the following way: what we invariably observe becoming different at different times—fire, for example—to characterize it, that is, fire, not as "this," but each time as "what is such," and speak of water not as "this," but always as "what is such." And never to speak of anything else as "this," as though it has some stability, of all the
e things at which we point and use the expressions "that" and

---

53. Literally "this thing itself," a reference to the Receptacle. The "preliminary problem" concerning fire and the others is raised in b7–d3 and a solution is proposed at d3–e7. The solution then provides the correct way of thinking and speaking of the Receptacle (e7–50a4).

54. The qualification is necessary, for it will turn out that earth cannot be transformed into the other three, and vice versa. See below, 54b–d.

"this" and so think we are designating something. For it gets away without abiding the charge of "that" and "this," or any other expression that indicts them of being stable. It is in fact safest not to refer to it by any of these expressions. Rather, "what is such"—coming around like what it was, again and again—*that's* the thing to call it in each and every case. So fire, and generally everything that has becoming, it is safest to call "what is altogether such." But that *in* which they each appear to keep coming to be and *from* which they subsequently perish, *that's* the 50 only thing to refer to by means of the expressions "that" and "this." A thing that is some "such" or other, however,—hot or white, say, or any one of the opposites, and all things constituted by these—should be called none of these things [i.e., "this" or "that"].[55]

I must make one more effort to describe it, more clearly still. Suppose you were molding gold into every shape there is, going on nonstop remolding one shape into the next. If someone then were to point at one of them and ask you, "What *is* it?," your *b* safest answer by far, with respect to truth, would be to say, "gold," but never "triangle" or any of the other shapes that come to be in the gold, as though it *is* these, because they change even while you're making the statement. However, that answer, too, should be satisfactory, as long as the shapes are willing to accept "what is such" as someone's designation. This has a degree of safety.

Now the same account holds also for that nature which receives all the bodies. We must always refer to it by the same term, for it does not depart from its own character in any way. Not only does it always receive all things, it has never in any way *c* whatever taken on any characteristic similar to any of the things that enter it. Its nature is to be available for anything to make its impression upon, and it is modified, shaped, and reshaped by the things that enter it. These are the things that make it appear different at different times. The things that enter and leave it are imitations of those things that always are, imprinted after their likeness in a marvelous way that is hard to describe. This is something we shall pursue at another time. For the moment, we need to keep in mind three types of things: that which comes to *d* be, that in which it comes to be, and that after which the thing

---

55. The translation of the passage 49c7–50a4 is controversial. An alternative translation, given and discussed in the Introduction (pp. lvi–lix), is preferred by many scholars.

coming to be is modeled and which is the source of its coming
to be. It is quite appropriate to compare the receiving thing to a
mother, the source to a father, and the nature between them to
their offspring. We also must understand that if the imprints are
to be varied, with all the varieties there to see, this thing upon
which the imprints are to be formed could not be well prepared
for that role if it were not itself devoid of any of those characters
e   that it is to receive from elsewhere. For if it resembled any of the
things that enter it, it could not successfully copy their opposites
or things of a totally different nature whenever it were to receive
them. It would be showing its own face as well. This is why the
thing that is to receive in itself all the [elemental] kinds must be
totally devoid of any characteristics. Think of people who make
fragrant ointments. They expend skill and ingenuity to come up
with something just like this [i.e., a neutral base], to have on hand
to start with. The liquids that are to receive the fragrances they
make as odorless as possible. Or think of people who work at
impressing shapes upon soft materials. They emphatically refuse
to allow any such material to already have some definite shape.
51   Instead, they'll even it out and make it as smooth as it can be. In
the same way, then, if the thing that is to receive repeatedly
throughout its whole self the likenesses of the intelligible objects,
the things which always are[56]—if it is to do so successfully, then
it ought to be devoid of any inherent characteristics of its own.
This, of course, is the reason why we shouldn't call the mother
or receptacle of what has come to be, of what is visible or perceiv-
able in every other way, either earth or air, fire, or water, or any
of their compounds or their constituents. But if we speak of it as
an invisible and characterless sort of thing, one that receives all
b   things and shares in a most perplexing way in what is intelligible,
a thing extremely difficult to comprehend, we shall not be misled.
And insofar as it is possible to arrive at its nature on the basis of
what we've said so far, the most correct way to speak of it may
well be this: the part of it that gets ignited appears on each occasion
as fire, the dampened part as water, and parts as earth or air
insofar as they receive the imitations of these.

But we must prefer to conduct our inquiry by means of rational
argument. Hence we should make a distinction like the following:
Is there such a thing as a Fire *by itself*? Do all these things of
c   which we always say that each of them is something "by itself"

---

56. Accepting the insertion of *noētōn* before *pantōn*.

really exist? Or are the things we see, and whatever else we perceive through the body, the only things that possess this kind of actuality, so that there is absolutely nothing else besides them at all? Is our perpetual claim that there exists an intelligible Form for each thing a vacuous gesture, in the end nothing but mere talk? Now we certainly will not do justice to the question before us if we dismiss it, leaving it undecided and unadjudicated, and just insist that such things exist, but neither must we append a further lengthy digression to a discourse already quite long. If,   *d* however, a significant distinction formulated in few words were to present itself, that would suit our present needs best of all. So here's how I cast my own vote: If understanding and true opinion are distinct, then these "by themselves" things definitely exist— these Forms, the objects not of our sense perception, but of our understanding only. But if—as some people think—true opinion does not differ in any way from understanding, then all the things we perceive through our bodily senses must be assumed to be the most stable things there are. But we do have to speak of   *e* understanding and true opinion as distinct, of course, because we can come to have one without the other, and the one is not like the other. It is through instruction that we come to have understanding, and through persuasion that we come to have true belief. Understanding always involves a true account, while true belief lacks any account. And while understanding remains unmoved by persuasion, true belief gives in to persuasion. And of true belief, it must be said, all men have a share, but of under-standing, only the gods and a small group of people do.

Since these things are so, we must agree that that which keeps   52 its own form unchangingly, which has not been brought into being and is not destroyed, which neither receives into itself anything else from anywhere else, nor itself enters into anything else anywhere, is one thing. It is invisible—it cannot be perceived by the senses at all—and it is the role of understanding to study it. The second thing is that which shares the other's name and resembles it. This thing can be perceived by the senses, and it has been begotten. It is constantly borne along, now coming to be in a certain place and then perishing out of it. It is apprehended by opinion, which involves sense perception. And the third type is space, which exists always and cannot be destroyed. It provides   *b* a fixed site for all things that come to be. It is itself apprehended by a kind of bastard reasoning that does not involve sense percep-tion, and it is hardly even an object of conviction [*pistis*]. We look

at it as in a dream when we say that everything that exists must
of necessity be somewhere, in some place and occupying some
space, and that that which doesn't exist somewhere, whether on
earth or in heaven, doesn't exist at all.

We prove unable to draw all these distinctions and others
related to them—even in the case of that unsleeping, truly existing
c reality—because our dreaming state renders us incapable of waking up and stating the truth, which is this: Since an image does
not have as its own that which it has come to signify (an image
is invariably borne along to depict *something else*), it stands to
reason that the image should therefore come to be *in* something
else, somehow clinging to being, or else be nothing at all. But
that which really is receives support from the accurate, true account: that as long as the one is distinct from the other, neither
d of them ever comes to be in the other in such a way that they at
the same time become one and the same, and also two.[57]

Let this, then, be a summary of the account I would offer, as
computed by my "vote." There are being, space, and becoming,
three distinct things that existed even before the heavens came
to be.

Now as the wetnurse of becoming turns[58] watery and fiery
and receives the character of earth and air, and as it acquires all
e the properties that come with these characters, it takes on a variety
of visible aspects, but because it is filled with powers that are
neither similar nor evenly balanced, no part of it is in balance. It
sways irregularly in every direction as it is shaken by those things,
and being set in motion it in turn shakes them. And as they are
moved, they drift continually, some in one direction and others

---

57. Plato's argument in this terse paragraph seems to be the following: If A
"signifies" B (in the sense of being an image of B), then it cannot be in itself what
B is—for then it would be B, not an image of B. And if it cannot be B, it must be
something else—something, whatever it is, that will sustain A's role and status
as an image of B. For example, a marble statue of a man cannot itself be a man,
otherwise it wouldn't be a *statue* of a man. So in order to be a *statue* of a man, it
must be something else intrinsically—marble, for instance—that sustains its role
and status as an image. So the image must be "in" marble. Images that aren't
"in" or "on" anything are "nothing at all." The final sentence reasserts the absence
of the "being in" relation (and perhaps by extension the "being of" relation)
between the model (Forms) and the subject (Receptacle): whereas the image is
"in" the latter (and "of" the former), they neither are "of" nor "in" each other.

58. Timaeus continues the discourse in the present tense at this point, dramatically
presenting the events as though we are invited to be spectators of them with him.

in others, separating from one another. They are winnowed out, as it were, like grain that is sifted by winnowing sieves or other such implements. They are carried off and settle down, the dense 53 and heavy ones in one direction, and the rare and light ones to another place.

That is how at that time the four kinds were being shaken by the receiver, which was itself agitating like a shaking machine, separating the kinds most unlike each other furthest apart and pushing those most like each other closest together into the same region. This, of course, explains how these different kinds came to occupy different regions of space, even before the universe was set in order and constituted from them. Indeed, it is a fact that before this took place the four kinds all lacked proportion and measure, and at the time the ordering of the universe was *b* undertaken, fire, water, earth, and air initially possessed certain traces of what they are now. They were indeed in the condition one would expect thoroughly god-forsaken things to be in. So, finding them in this natural condition, the first thing the god then did was to give them their distinctive shapes, using forms and numbers.

Here is a proposition we shall always affirm above all else: *The god fashioned these four kinds to be as perfect and excellent as possible, when they were not so before.* It will now be my task to explain to you what structure each of them acquired, and how each came to be. My account will be an unusual one, but since *c* you are well schooled in the fields of learning in terms of which I must of necessity proceed with my exposition, I'm sure you'll follow me.

First of all, everyone knows, I'm sure, that fire, earth, water, and air are bodies. Now everything that has bodily form also has depth. Depth, moreover, is of necessity comprehended within surface, and any surface bounded by straight lines is composed of triangles. Every triangle, moreover, derives from two triangles, *d* each of which has one right angle and two acute angles. Of these two triangles, one [the isosceles right-angled triangle] has at each of the other two vertices an equal part of a right angle, determined by its division by equal sides; while the other [the scalene right-angled triangle] has unequal parts of a right angle at its other two vertices, determined by the division of the right angle by unequal sides. This, then, we presume to be the originating principle [*archē*] of fire and of the other bodies, as we pursue our likely account in terms of Necessity. Principles yet more ultimate than these are known only to the god, and to any man he may hold dear.

e   We should now say which are the most excellent four bodies that can come to be. They are quite unlike each other, though some of them are capable of breaking up and turning into others and vice versa. If our account is on the mark, we shall have the truth about how earth and fire and their proportionate intermediates [water and air] came to be. For we shall never concede to anyone that there are any visible bodies more excellent than these, each conforming to a single kind. So we must wholeheartedly proceed to fit together the four kinds of bodies of surpassing excellence, and to declare that we have come to grasp their natures well enough.

54   Of the two [right-angled] triangles, the isosceles has but one nature, while the scalene has infinitely many. Now we have to select the most excellent one from among the infinitely many, if we are to get a proper start. So if anyone can say that he has picked out another one that is more excellent for the construction of these bodies, his victory will be that of a friend, not an enemy. Of the many [scalene right-angled] triangles, then, we posit as the one most excellent, surpassing the others, that one from [a pair of] which the equilateral triangle is constructed as a third

b   figure. Why this is so is too long a story to tell now. But if anyone puts this claim to the test and discovers that it isn't so, his be the prize, with our congratulations. So much, then, for the selection of the two triangles out of which the bodies of fire and the other bodies are constructed—the [right-angled] isosceles, and [the right-angled] scalene whose longer side squared is always triple its shorter side squared [i.e., the half-equilateral].[59]

At this point we need to formulate more precisely something that was not stated clearly earlier. For then it appeared that all four kinds of bodies could turn into one another by successive

c   stages. But the appearance is wrong.[60] While there are indeed four kinds of bodies that come to be from the [right-angled] triangles we have selected, three of them come from triangles that have unequal sides, whereas the fourth alone is fashioned out of isosceles triangles. Thus not all of them have the capacity of breaking

---

59. For analysis and discussion of this argument in 53c–54b, see the Introduction, pp. lxvi–lxvii.

60. Compare 49b–c and n. 54. See the Introduction, p. lxix.

up and turning into one another, with a large number of small bodies turning into a small number of large ones and vice versa. There are three that can do this. For all three are made up of a single type of triangle, so that when once the larger bodies are broken up, the same triangles can go to make up a large number of small bodies, assuming shapes appropriate to them. And likewise, when numerous small bodies are fragmented into their triangles,   *d* these triangles may well combine to make up some single massive body belonging to another kind.

So much, then, for our account of how these bodies turn into one another. Let us next discuss the form that each of them has come to have, and the various numbers that have combined to make them up.

Leading the way will be the primary form, the tiniest structure,[61] whose elementary triangle is the one whose hypotenuse is twice the length of its shorter side. Now when a pair of such triangles are juxtaposed along the diagonal [i.e., their hypotenuses] and this is done three times, and their diagonals and short   *e* sides converge upon a single point as center, the result is a single equilateral triangle, composed of six such triangles.[62] When four of these equilateral triangles are combined, a single solid angle is produced at the junction of three plane angles. This, it turns   55 out, is the angle that comes right after the most obtuse of the plane angles.[63] And once four such solid angles have been completed, we get the primary solid form, which is one that divides the entire

---

61. The tetrahedron.

62. Juxtaposing AOD and AOE along their common side AO, and similarly BOD and BOF along BO, and COE and COF along CO, then joining the resulting trapezia at O.

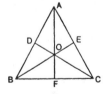

A pair of such triangles juxtaposed along the longer of the two sides enclosing the right angle will also produce an equilateral triangle (e.g., if ADO and AEO were juxtaposed along AE/AD). It is not clear why Plato does not propose this as a simpler construction. See the Introduction, n. 141.

63. That is, the conjunction of three 60° angles, totaling 180°. All obtuse angles are <180°. For another way of construing this sentence, see Popper [87].

circumference [sc. of the sphere in which it is inscribed] into equal and similar parts.

The second solid form[64] is constructed out of the same [elementary] triangles, which, however, are now arranged in eight equilateral triangles, and produce a single solid angle out of four plane angles. And when six such solid angles have been produced, the second body has reached its completion.

Now the third body[65] is made up of a combination of one
b hundred and twenty of the elementary triangles, and of twelve solid angles, each enclosed by five plane equilateral triangles. This body turns out to have twenty equilateral triangular faces. And let us take our leave of this one of the elementary triangles, the one that has begotten the above three kinds of bodies, and turn to the other one, the isosceles [right-angled] triangle, which has begotten the fourth.[66] Arranged in sets of four whose right angles come together at the center, the isosceles triangle produced a single equilateral quadrangle [i.e., a square]. And when six
c of these quadrangles were combined, they produced eight solid angles, each of which was constituted by three plane right angles. The shape of the resulting body so constructed is a cube, and it has six quadrangular equilateral faces.

One other construction, a fifth, still remained, and this one the god used for the whole universe, embroidering figures on it.[67]

Anyone following this whole line of reasoning might very

---

64. The octahedron, produced by joining four equilateral triangles to form a solid angle, will require eight such triangles joined at six solid angles for its completion. For diagrams of this and the other polyhedra, see the Introduction, p. lxvii.

65. The icosahedron, produced by joining five equilateral triangles to form a solid angle. It requires 120 elemental "perfect" scalene right-angled triangles, arranged in 20 equilateral triangles—see n. 62 above—joined at 12 solid angles for its completion.

66. The cube, made up of squares, produced by juxtaposing AOB, BOC, COD, and AOD at O.

Again (cf. n. 62 above), it is not clear why Plato does not construct the square out of two isosceles right-angled triangles, for example, AOD and DOC, juxtaposed at AD/DC.

67. The dodecahedron, the remaining one of the regular solids. It has twelve faces, each of which is a regular pentagon. This solid cannot be constructed out

well be puzzled about whether we should say that there are infinitely many worlds or a finite number of them. If so, he would have to conclude that to answer "infinitely many" is to take the view of one who is really "unfinished" in things he ought to be "finished" in.[68] He would do better to stop with the question whether we should say that there's really just one world or five and be puzzled about that. Well, our "likely account" answer declares there to be but one world, a god—though someone else, taking other things into consideration, will come to a different opinion. We must set him aside, however.

 Let us now assign to fire, earth, water, and air the structures that have just been given their formations in our speech. To earth let us give the cube, because of the four kinds of bodies earth is the most immobile and the most pliable—which is what the solid whose faces are the most secure must of necessity turn out to be, more so than the others. Now of the [right-angled] triangles we originally postulated, the face belonging to those that have equal sides has a greater natural stability than that belonging to triangles that have unequal sides, and the surface that is composed of the two triangles, the equilateral quadrangle [the square], holds its position with greater stability than does the equilateral triangle, both in their parts and as wholes. Hence, if we assign this solid figure to earth, we are preserving our "likely account." And of the solid figures that are left, we shall next assign the least mobile of them to water, to fire the most mobile, and to air the one in between. This means that the tiniest body belongs to fire, the largest to water, and the intermediate one to air—and also that the body with the sharpest edges belongs to fire, the next sharpest to air, and the third sharpest to water. Now in all these cases the body that has the fewest faces is of necessity the most mobile, in that it, more than any other, has edges that are the sharpest and best fit for cutting in every direction. It is also the lightest, in that it is made up of the least number of identical parts. The second body ranks second in having these same properties, and the third ranks third. So let us follow our account, which is not only likely but also correct, and take the solid form of the pyramid that we saw constructed as the element or the seed of fire. And let us say

d

e

56

b

---

of either of the two elemental right-angled triangles. It approaches most nearly a sphere in volume—the shape of the universe, according to Timaeus.

68. Plato is punning on *apeiros,* which on the one hand means "infinite" or "indefinite," and on the other, "inexperienced."

that the second form in order of generation is that of air, and the
third that of water.

Now we must think of all these bodies as being so small that
c due to their small size none of them, whatever their kind, is visible
to us individually. When, however, a large number of them are
clustered together, we do see them in bulk. And in particular, as
to the proportions among their numbers, their motions, and their
other properties, we must think that when the god had brought
them to complete and exact perfection (to the degree that Necessity was willing to comply obediently), he arranged them together
proportionately.

Given all we have said so far about the kinds of elemental
d bodies, the following account [of their transformations] is the
most likely: When earth encounters fire and is broken up by fire's
sharpness, it will drift about—whether the breaking up occurred
within fire itself, or within a mass of air or water—until its parts
meet again somewhere, refit themselves together, and become
earth again. The reason is that the parts of earth will never pass
into another form. But when water is broken up into parts by fire
or even by air, it could happen that the parts recombine to form
e one corpuscle of fire and two of air. And the fragments of air
could produce, from any single particle that is broken up, two
fire corpuscles. And conversely, whenever a small amount of fire
is enveloped by a large quantity of air or water or perhaps earth
and is agitated inside them as they move, and in spite of its
resistance is beaten and shattered to bits, then any two fire corpuscles may combine to constitute a single form of air. And when
air is overpowered and broken down, then two and a half entire
forms of air will be consolidated into a single, entire form of
water.[69]

Let us recapitulate and formulate our account of these transformations as follows: Whenever one of the other kinds is caught
57 inside fire and gets cut up by the sharpness of fire's angles and
edges, then if it is reconstituted as fire, it will stop getting cut.

---

69. A corpuscle (*sōma*) of water is an icosahedron, consisting of 20 equilateral
triangles or 120 elementary triangles, sufficient to constitute one tetrahedron (4
eq. or 24 el. triangles) and two octahedra (8 eq. or 48 el. triangles each). A corpuscle
of air is an octahedron, and so sufficient to constitute two tetrahedra. Conversely,
two fire corpuscles have the required constituent triangles to make up one of air,
and two and a half air corpuscles can make up a water corpuscle (or perhaps
better: five air corpuscles can make up two of water). See Vlastos [41], pp. 70–73.
Plato seems to use "corpuscle" and "form" (*eidos*) interchangeably in this passage.

The reason is that a thing of any kind that is alike and uniform is incapable of effecting any change in, or being affected by, anything that is similar to it. But as long as something involved in a transformation has something stronger than it to contend with, the process of its dissolution will continue nonstop. And likewise, when a few of the smaller corpuscles are surrounded *b* by a greater number of bigger ones, they will be shattered and quenched. The quenching will stop when these smaller bodies are willing to be reconstituted into the form of the kind that prevailed over them, and so from fire will come air, and from air, water. But if these smaller corpuscles are in process of turning into these and one of the other kinds encounters them and engages them in battle, their dissolution will go on nonstop until they are either completely squeezed and broken apart and escape to their own likes, or else are defeated, and, melding from many into one, they are assimilated to the kind that prevailed over them, and come to share its abode from then on. And what is more, as they *c* undergo these processes, they all exchange their territories: for as a result of the Receptacle's agitation the masses of each of the kinds are separated from one another, with each occupying its own region, but because some parts of a particular kind do from time to time become unlike their former selves and like the other kinds, they are carried by the shaking toward the region occupied by whatever masses they are becoming like to.

These, then, are the sorts of causes by which the unalloyed primary bodies have come to be. Now the fact that different varieties are found within their respective forms is to be attributed to the constructions of each of the elementary triangles. Each of *d* these two constructions did not originally yield a triangle that had just one size, but triangles that were both smaller and larger, numerically as many as there are varieties within a given form. That is why when they are mixed with themselves and with each other, they display an infinite variety, which those who are to employ a likely account in their study of nature ought to take note of.

Now as for motion and rest, unless there is agreement on the manner and the conditions in which these two come to be, we will have many obstacles to face in our subsequent course of *e* reasoning. Although we have already said something about them, we need to say this as well: *there will be no motion in a state of uniformity.* For it is difficult, or rather impossible, for something to be moved without something to set it in motion, or something

to set a thing in motion without something to be moved by it. When either is absent, there is no motion, but [when they are present] it is quite impossible for them to be uniform. And so let us always presume that rest is found in a state of uniformity and
58 to attribute motion to nonuniformity. The latter, moreover, is caused by inequality, the origin of which we have already discussed.[70]

We have not explained, however, how it is that the various corpuscles have not reached the point of being thoroughly separated from each other kind by kind, so that their transformations into each other and their movement [toward their own regions] would have come to a halt. So let us return to say this about it: Once the circumference of the universe has comprehended the [four] kinds, then, because it is round and has a natural tendency to gather in upon itself, it constricts them all and allows no empty
b space to be left over. This is why fire, more than the other three, has come to infiltrate all of the others, with air in second place, since it is second in degree of subtlety, and so on for the rest. For the bodies that are generated from the largest parts will have the largest gaps left over in their construction, whereas the smallest bodies will have the tiniest. Now this gathering, contracting process squeezes the small parts into the gaps inside the big ones. So now, as the small parts are placed among the large ones and the smaller ones tend to break up the larger ones while the larger tend to cause the smaller to coalesce, they all shift, up and down,
c into their own respective regions. For as each changes in quantity, it also changes the position of its region. This, then, is how and why the occurrence of nonuniformity is perpetually preserved, and so sets these bodies in perpetual motion, both now and in the future without interruption.

Next, we should note that there are many varieties of fire that have come to be. For example, there is both flame and the effluence from flame which, while it doesn't burn, gives light to the eyes.
d And then there is the residue of flame that is left in the embers when the flame has gone out. The same goes for air. There is the

---

70. The reference to the discussion of "the origin of inequality" is unclear. Perhaps Plato is thinking of the discussion of the "powers that are neither similar nor evenly balanced" (52e) in the primal chaos. Or perhaps, more specifically, he has in mind the origin of the differences among the elemental structures. These differences are due to the dissimilarity of the two primal triangles, their different sizes, and the different possible combinations and recombinations of the scalene right-angled triangles.

brightest kind that we call "aether," and also the murkiest, "mist" and "darkness." Then there are other, nameless sorts that result from inequality among the triangles. The varieties of water can first of all be divided into two groups, the liquid and the liquifiable. Because the former possesses water parts that are not only unequal but also small, it turns out to be mobile, both in itself and when acted upon by something else. This is due to its nonuniformity and the configuration of its shape. The other type of water, composed of large and uniform kinds, is rather more immobile and heavy, compacted as it is by its uniformity. But when fire penetrates it and begins to break it up, it loses its uniformity, and once that is lost, it is more susceptible to motion. When it has become quite mobile, it is spread out upon the ground under pressure from the air surrounding it. Each of these changes has its own name: "melting" for the disintegration of its bulk and "flowing" for the spreading on the ground. But when, conversely, the fire is expelled from it, then, since the fire does not pass into a void, pressure is exerted upon the surrounding air, which in turn compresses the still mobile liquid mass into the places previously occupied by the fire and mixes it with itself. As it is being compressed, the mass regains its uniformity now that fire, the agent of nonuniformity, has left the scene, and it resettles into its own former state. The departure of the fire is called "cooling," and the compression that occurs when the fire is gone is called "jelling." Of all these types of water that we have called liquifiable, the one that consists of the finest, the most uniform parts and has proved to be the most dense, one that is unique in its kind and tinged with brilliant yellow, is gold, our most precious possession, filtered through rocks and thereby compacted. And gold's offshoot, which because of its density is extremely hard and has a black color, is called adamant. Another has parts that approximate gold and comes in more than one variety. In terms of density, it is in one way denser than gold and includes a small, fine part of earth, so that it is harder. But it is actually lighter than gold, because it has large gaps inside of it. This, it turns out, is copper, one variety of the bright, jelled kinds of water. Whenever the earth part of the mixture separates off again from the rest in the passage of time, this part, called verdigris, becomes visible by itself.

As for going further and giving an account of other stuffs of this sort along the lines of the likely stories we have been following, that is no complicated matter. And should one take a break and lay aside accounts about the things that always are, deriving

d instead a carefree pleasure from surveying the likely accounts
about becoming, he would provide his life with a moderate and
sensible diversion. So shall we, then, at this time give free rein
to such a diversion and go right on to set out the next likelihoods
on these subjects, as follows.

Take now the water that is mixed with fire. It is fine and liquid
and on account of its mobility and the way it rolls over the ground
it is called "liquid." It is soft, moreover, in that its faces, being
less firm than those of earth, give way to it. When this water is
e separated from its fire and air and is isolated, it becomes more
uniform, and it is pressed together into itself by the things that
leave it. So compacted, the water above the earth which is most
affected by this change turns to hail, while that on earth turns to
ice. Some water is not affected quite so much, being still only half
compacted. Such water above the earth becomes snow, while
that on the earth becomes what is called "frost," from dew that
is congealed.

Now most of the varieties of water that are mixed with one
60 another are collectively called "saps," because they have been
filtered through plants that grow out of the earth. Because they
are mixed, each of them has its own degree of nonuniformity.
Many of these varieties are nameless, though four of them, all
with fire in them, are particularly conspicuous and so have been
given names. First, there is wine, which warms not only the body
but the soul as well. Second, there are the various oils, which are
smooth and divide [the ray of] sight and for that reason glisten,
appearing bright and shiny to the eye: these include resin, castor
b oil, olive oil, and others that share their properties. And third,
there is what is most commonly called honey, which includes all
that relaxes the taste passages of the mouth back to their natural
state, and which by virtue of this property conveys a sense of
sweetness. Fourth, there is what has been named tart juice, quite
distinct from all the other saps. It is a foamy stuff, and is caustic
and hence hazardous to the flesh.

As for the varieties of earth, first, such earth as has been filtered
through water turns into a stony body in something like the
following way: When the water that is mixed with it disintegrates
in the mixing process, it is transformed into the form of air, and,
c once it has turned into air, it thrusts its way upward toward its
own region. And since there is no void above it, it pushes aside
the air next to it. And when this air, heavy as it is, is pressed
and poured around the mass of earth, it squeezes it hard and

compresses it to fill the places vacated by the recently formed air. When so compressed by air, earth is insoluble in water and constitutes itself as stone. The more beautiful kind of stone is the kind that is transparent and made up of equal and uniform parts; the uglier kind is just the opposite. Second, there is the kind of earth from which moisture has been completely expelled by a swiftly burning fire and which thus comes to have a rather more brittle constitution than the first kind of earth. This is a kind to which the name "pottery" has been given. Sometimes, however, moisture gets left in and we get earth that is made liquifiable by fire. When it has cooled, it turns to stone that is black in color [i.e., lava]. Third, there are the two varieties of earth that, both alike, are the residue of a mixture of a great quantity of water. They are briny, made up of the finest parts of earth, and turn out to be semisolid and water soluble again. One of these is soda, a cleansing agent against oil and dirt; the other is salt, which is well suited to enhance various blends of flavor and has, not unreasonably, proven itself to be a stuff pleasing to the gods.

There are also compounds of earth and water which are soluble by fire but not by water.[71] These are compacted in this way for the following sort of reason: Neither air nor fire will dissolve masses of earth, because air and fire consist of parts that by nature are smaller than are the gaps within earth. They thus pass without constraint through the wide gaps of a mass of earth, leaving it intact and undissolved. But since the parts of water are naturally bigger, they must force their way through, and in so doing they undo and dissolve the earth. For water alone can in this way dissolve earth that isn't forcibly compressed, but when earth is compressed nothing but fire can dissolve it. That is because fire is the only thing left that can penetrate it. So also, only fire can disperse water that has been compressed with the greatest force, whereas both fire and air can disperse water that is in a looser state. Air does it by entering the gaps, and fire by breaking up the triangles. The only way in which air that has been condensed under force can be broken up is into its elemental [triangles], and even when it is not forcibly compressed only fire can dissolve it.

So as for these bodies that are mixtures of earth and water, as long as the gaps within a given mass of earth are occupied by its own water that is tightly packed within the gaps, the water parts that come charging upon it from the outside have no way

d

e

61

b

---

71. For example, glass, wax, and similar bodies; see below.

of getting into the mass and so flow around the whole of it, leaving it undissolved. The fire parts, however, do penetrate the gaps within the water parts and hence as fire they do to water[72] what water did to earth. They alone, it turns out, cause this body, this partnership of earth and water, to come apart and become fluid. These compounds of earth and water include not only bodies that have less water in them than earth, such as glass and generally all stone formations that can be called liquifiable, but

c   also bodies that have more water than earth, namely all those that have the consistency of wax or of incense.

   We have now pretty much completed our presentation of the kinds of bodies that are distinguished by their multifarious shapes, their combinations, and their intertransformations. Now we must try to shed some light on what has caused them to come to have the properties[73] they do. First, we need at every step in our discourse to appeal to the existence of sense perception, but we have so far discussed neither the coming to be of flesh, or of what pertains to flesh, nor the part of the soul that is mortal.[74] It

d   so happens, however, that we cannot give an adequate account of these matters without referring to perceptual properties, but neither can we give an account of the latter without referring to the former, and to treat them simultaneously is all but impossible. So we must start by assuming the one or the other, and later revisit what we have assumed. Let's begin by taking for granted for now the existence of body and soul. This will allow our account of these properties to succeed the account we've just given of the elemental kinds.

   First, then, let us see what we mean when we call fire *hot*. Let's look at it in this way: We notice how fire acts on our bodies

e   by dividing and cutting them. We are all well aware that the experience is a sharp one. The fineness of fire's edges, the sharpness of its angles, the minuteness of its parts, and the swiftness of its motion—all of which make fire severely piercing, so that it

62   makes sharp cuts in whatever it encounters—must be taken into consideration as we recall how its shape came to be. It is this substance, more than any other, that divides our bodies through-

---

72. Accepting the conjecture *hudōr* at b5. See Cornford [14], p. 257, n. 1.

73. For Plato's use of *pathēma* and *pathos* and my translation of these terms here and in various contexts to follow, see the Introduction, p. lxxv and n. 147.

74. The mortal soul will be discussed at 69c–72d; the body parts and systems at 72d–81e.

out and cuts them up into small pieces, thereby giving us the property (as well as the name[75]) that we now naturally call *hot*.

What the opposite property is, is quite obvious; we should not, however, keep anything left out of our account. As the larger parts of the moisture surrounding our bodies penetrate our bodies and push out the smaller parts but are unable to take up the places vacated by those smaller parts, they compress the moisture *b* within us and congeal it by rendering it in a state of motionlessness in place of a state of moving nonuniformity, by virtue of the uniformity and compression so introduced. But anything that is being unnaturally compressed has a natural tendency to resist such compression, and pushes itself outward, in the opposite direction. This resistance, this shaking, is called "shivering" and "chill," and the experience as a whole, as well as what brings it about, has come to have the name *cold*.

Hard we call whatever our flesh gives way to; *soft*, whatever gives way to our flesh. And this is how they are relative to each other. Whatever stands upon a small base tends to give way. The form composed of quadrangles, however, is the least liable to *c* being displaced because its bases are very secure, and that which is compacted to its maximum density is particularly resistant to being displaced.

Heavy and *light* can be most clearly explained if we examine them in conjunction with what we call *above* and *below*. It is entirely wrong to hold that there are by nature two separate regions, divorced from and entirely opposite to one another, the one the region "below," toward which anything that has physical mass tends to move, and the other the region "above," toward which everything makes its way only under force. For given that the whole heaven is spherical, all the points that are situated as ex- *d* tremes at an equal distance from the center must by their nature be extremes of just the same sort, and we must take it that the center, being equidistant from the extremes, is situated at the point that is the opposite to all the extremes. Now if this is the world's natural constitution, which of the points just mentioned could you posit as "above" or "below" without justly giving the appearance of using totally inappropriate language? There is no justification for describing the world's central region either as a natural "above" or a natural "below," but just as "at the center."

---

75. Plato here implies an etymology connecting *kermatizein* ("to cut up into small pieces") and *thermon* ("hot").

And the region at the circumference is, to be sure, not the center, but neither is one of its parts so distinguished from any other that it is related to the center [in a specific way] more so than any of the parts opposite to it. What contrary terms could you apply to something that is by nature all alike in every direction? How could you think to use such terms appropriately? If, further,
63   there is something solid and evenly balanced at the center of the universe, it could not move to any of the extreme points, because these are all alike in all directions. But if you could travel around it in a circle, you would repeatedly take a position at your own antipodes and call the very same part of it now the part "above," and then the part "below." For the whole universe, as we have just said, is spherical, and to say that some region of it is its "above," and another its "below," makes no sense. The origin of these terms and the subjects to which they really apply, which explain how we have become accustomed to using them in divid-
b   ing the world as a whole in this way, we must resolve by adopting the following supposition: Imagine a man stepping onto that region of the universe which is the particular province of fire, where the greatest mass of fire is gathered together, and toward which other fire moves. Imagine, further, that he has the power to remove some parts of the fire and place them on scales. When he raises the beam and drags the fire into the alien air, applying
c   force to it, clearly the lesser quantity [of fire] somehow gives way to his force more easily than the greater. For when two things are raised by one and the same exertion, the lesser quantity will invariably yield more readily and the greater (which offers more resistance) less readily, to the force applied. And so the large quantity will be described as *heavy* and moving *downward*, and the small one as *light* and moving *upward*. Now this is the very thing we must detect ourselves doing in our own region. When we stand on the earth and weigh out one earth-like thing against another, and sometimes some earth itself, we drag these things by force, contrary to their natural tendency, into the alien air.
d   While both of them tend to cling to what is akin to them, neverthe-less the smaller one will yield sooner and more readily than the larger one to the force we apply that introduces it into the alien stuff. Now this is what we call *light*, and the region into which we force it to go we call *above*; their opposites we call *heavy* and *below*. Now the things [having any of these designations] necessarily differ relatively to one another, because the various masses of the elemental kinds of body occupy opposite regions: what in one region is light, heavy, below, or above will all be

found to become, or to be, directly opposite to, or at an angle to,   *e*
or in any and every different direction from, what is light, heavy,
below, or above in the opposite region. In fact, this is the one
thing that should be understood to apply in all these cases: the
path toward its own kind is what makes a thing moving along
it "heavy" and the region into which it moves, "below," whereas
the other set of terms ["light" and "above"] are for things behaving
the other way. This, then, concludes our account of what causes
[things to have] these properties.

As for *smooth* and *rough*, I take it that anyone could discern
the explanation of those properties and communicate it to someone else: roughness results from the combination of hardness with
nonuniformity, while smoothness is the result of uniformity's   64
contribution to density.

The most important point that remains concerning the properties that have a common effect upon the body as a whole[76] pertains
to the causes of pleasures and pains in the cases we have described
as well as all cases in which sensations are registered throughout
the bodily parts, sensations that are simultaneously accompanied
by pains and pleasures in those parts. With every property,
whether perceived or not, let us take up the question of the causes
of pleasure or pain in the following way, recalling the distinction   *b*
made in the foregoing between what is easily moved and what
is hard to move. This is the way in which we must pursue all
that we intend to comprehend. When even a minor disturbance
affects that which is easily moved by nature, the disturbance is
passed on in a chain reaction[77] with some parts affecting others
in the same way as they were affected, until it reaches the center
of consciousness and reports the property that produced the reaction. On the other hand, something that is hard to move remains
fixed and merely experiences the disturbance without passing it
on in any chain reaction. It does not disturb any of its neighboring   *c*
parts, so that in the absence of some parts passing on the disturbance to others, the initial disturbance affecting them fails to move
on into the living thing as a whole and renders the disturbance
unperceived. This is true of our bones and hair and of the other
mostly earth-made parts that we possess. But the former is true
of our sight and hearing in particular, and this is because their
chief inherent power is that of air and of fire.

---

76. That is, that affect via the sense of touch any part of the body, as the previously
considered pairs hot-cold, hard-soft, heavy-light, smooth-rough do.

77. Literally, "in a cycle."

d   This, then, is what we should understand about pleasure and pain: an unnatural disturbance that comes upon us with great force and intensity is painful, while its equally intense departure, leading back to the natural state, is pleasant. One that is mild and gradual is not perceived, whereas the opposite is the case with the opposite disturbance. Further, one that occurs readily can be completely perceived, more so than any other, though neither pleasure nor pain is involved. Take, for example, those involved in the act of seeing. Earlier[78] we described [the ray of] sight as a body that comes into being with the daylight as an extension of ourselves. The cuttings, the burnings, and whatever else it

e   undergoes don't cause any pains in it, nor does the return to its former state yield any pleasures. Its perceptions are the more vivid and clear the more it is affected and the greater the number of things it encounters and makes contact with, for there is absolutely no violence involved when it is severed [by the cutting and burning, etc.] and reconstituted. Bodies consisting of larger parts, on the other hand, won't easily give way to what acts upon them. They pass on the motions they receive to the entire body, and so they do get pleasures and pains—pains when they are alienated

65   from their natural condition and pleasures when they are once again restored to it. All those bodies that experience only gradual departures from their normal state or gradual depletions but whose replenishments are intense and substantial are bodies that are unaware of their depletions but not of their replenishments, and hence they introduce very substantial pleasures in the mortal part of the soul but not any pains. This is clear in the case of fragrances. But all those bodies whose alienations are intense

b   while their restorations to their former states are but gradual and slow pass on motions that are entirely contrary to those mentioned just before. Again, this clearly turns out to be the case when the body suffers burns or cuts.

       We have now pretty much covered those disturbances that affect the whole body in a common way, as well as all the terms that have come to be applied to the agents that produce them. We must now try to discuss, if we can, those that take place in our various particular parts, and, as before, their causes, which

c   lie in the agents that produce them. First, then, we need to shed what light we can on what we left untreated earlier when we talked about tastes, and these are the properties specifically con-

---

78. At 45c.

nected to the tongue. It seems that these, too, in common with most other properties, come about as a result of contractions and dilations, but apart from that, these tongue-related properties seem rather more than any of the others to involve roughness and smoothness. Now as earth-like parts penetrate the area around the tiny vessels that act as testers for the tongue and reach down to the heart, they impact upon the moist, soft flesh of the tongue and are melted away. In the process they contract the vessels and dry them up. When they tend to be rather rough, we taste them as *sour*; when less rough, as *tangy*. Things that rinse the vessels and wash the entire area around the tongue are all called *bitter* when they do so to excess and so assault the tongue as to dissolve some of it, as soda actually can do. When they are not as strong as soda and effect only a moderate rinsing, they taste *salty* to us. They have none of the harsh bitterness, and we find them rather agreeable. Things that absorb the heat of the mouth, by which they are also worn smooth, are ignited and in their turn return their fire to that which made them hot. Their lightness carries them up to the senses in the head, as they cut any and everything they come up against. Because this is what they do, things of this sort have all been called *pungent*. On the other hand, there are those things[79] that have been refined by the process of decomposition and that then intrude themselves into the narrow vessels. These are proportioned both to the earth parts and those of air that are contained within the vessels, so that [when they intrude themselves,] they agitate the earth and air parts and cause them to be stirred one around the other. As these are being stirred, they surround one another, and, as parts of one sort intrude themselves into parts of another, they make hollows that envelop the parts that go inside. So when a hollow envelope of moisture, whether earthy or pure, as the case may be, is stretched around air, we get moist vessels of air, hollow spheres of water. Some of these, those that form a transparent enclosure consisting of a pure moisture, are called "bubbles"; those, on the other hand, whose moisture is earthy and agitates and rises upward all at once are called by the terms "effervescence" and "fermentation." That which causes these disturbances is called *acid* to the taste.

There is a disturbance that is the opposite of all the ones we have just discussed, one that is the effect of an opposite cause. Whenever the composition of the moistened parts that enter the

d

e

66

b

c

---

79. The text is uncertain here.

vessels of the tongue is such that it is congruent with the natural condition of the tongue, these entering parts make smooth and lubricate the roughened parts and in some cases constrict while in others they relax the parts that have been abnormally dilated or contracted. They decisively restore all those parts back to their natural position. As such, they prove to be a cure for the violent disturbances [just discussed], being fully pleasant and agreeable to one and all, and are called *sweet.*

d   So much for the subject of tastes. As for the power belonging to the nostrils, there are no types within it. This is because a smell is always a "half-breed." None of the elemental shapes, as it happens, has the proportions required for having any odor. The vessels involved in our sense of smell are too narrow for the varieties of earth and water parts, yet too wide for those of fire and air. Consequently no one has ever perceived any odor coming from these elemental bodies. Things give off odors when they

e   either get damp or decay, or melt or evaporate; for when water changes to air or air to water, odors are given off in the transition. All odors collectively are either vapor or mist, mist being what passes from air to water, and vapor what passes from water to air, and this is why odors as a group turn out to be finer than water, yet grosser than air. Their character becomes clear when one strains to draw one's breath through something that obstructs one's breathing. There will be no odor that filters through. All that comes through is just the breath itself, devoid of any odor.

67   These variations among odors, then, form two sets, neither of which has a name, since they do not consist of a specific number of simple types. Let us draw the only clear distinction we can draw here, that between the *pleasant* and the *offensive.* The latter of these irritates and violates the whole upper body from the top of the head to the navel, while the former soothes that area and welcomes it back to its natural state.

b   A third kind of perception that we want to consider is hearing. We must describe the causes that produce the properties connected with this perception. In general, let us take it that sound is the percussion of air by way of the ears upon the brain and the blood and transmitted to the soul, and that hearing is the motion caused by the percussion that begins in the head and ends in the place where the liver is situated. And let us take it that whenever the percussion is rapid, the sound is *high-pitched,* and that the slower the percussion, the lower the pitch. A regular percussion produces a uniform, smooth sound, while a contrary

c   one produces one that is *rough.* A forceful percussion produces a *loud* sound, while a contrary one produces one that is *soft*. But we must defer discussion of harmonization in sounds to a later part of our discourse.

The fourth and remaining kind of perception is one that includes a vast number of variations within it, and hence it requires subdivision. Collectively, we call these variations *colors*. Color is a flame that flows forth from bodies of all sorts, with its parts proportional to our sight so as to produce perception. At an earlier point in our discourse we treated only the causes that led to the origination of [the ray of] sight;[80] now, at this point, it is particularly appropriate to provide a well-reasoned account of colors.   *d*

Now the parts that move from the other objects and impinge on the ray of sight are in some cases smaller, in others larger than, and in still other cases equal in size to, the parts of the ray of sight itself. Those that are equal are imperceptible, and these we naturally call *transparent*. Those that are larger contract the ray of sight, while those that are smaller, on the other hand, dilate it, and so are "cousin" to what is cold or hot in the case of the flesh, and, in the case of the tongue, to what is sour, or to all   *e* those things that generate heat and that we have therefore called "pungent." So *black* and *white*, it turns out, are properties of contraction and dilation, and are really the same as these other properties, though in a different class, which is why they present a different appearance. This, then, is how we should speak of them: *white* is what dilates the ray of sight, and *black* is what does the opposite.

Now when a more penetrating motion of a different type of fire pounces on the ray of sight and dilates it right up to the eyes, and forces its way through the very passages within the eyeballs   *68* and melts them, it discharges from those passages a glob of fire and water which we call a tear. The penetrating motion itself consists of fire, and as it encounters fire from the opposite direction, then, as the one fire leaps out from the eyes like a lightning flash and the other enters them but is quenched by the surrounding moisture, the resulting turmoil gives rise to colors of every hue. The disturbance so produced we call "dazzling," and that which produces it we name *bright* and *brilliant*.

On the other hand, the type of fire that is intermediate between   *b* white and bright is one that reaches the moisture in the eyes and blends with it but is not brilliant. As the fire shines through the moisture with which it is mixed, it yields the color of blood, which

---

80. See 45b–d.

we call *red*. And when bright is mixed with red and white, we get *orange*. But it would be unwise to state the proportions among them, even if one could know them. It is impossible, even approximately, to provide a proof or a likely account on these matters.

c   Now red mixed with black and white is of course *purple*. When this combination is burnt further and more black is mixed with it, we get *violet*. *Gray* is a mixture of black and white, and the mixture of orange and gray produces *amber*. *Beige* comes from white mixed with orange. White combined with bright and immersed in a saturated black produces a *cobalt blue* color, which, when blended with white, becomes *turquoise*. A mixture of amber

d   with black yields *green*. As for the other hues, it should be fairly clear from the above cases by what mixtures they are to be represented in a way that preserves our "likely story." But if anyone who in considering these matters were to put them to an actual test, he would demonstrate his ignorance of the difference between the human and the divine. It is god who possesses both the knowledge and power required to mix a plurality into a unity and, conversely, to dissolve a unity into a plurality, while no human being could possess either of these, whether at the present time or at any time in the future.

e   And so all these things were taken in hand, their natures being determined then by Necessity in the way we've described, by the craftsman of the most perfect and excellent among things that come to be, at the time when he brought forth that self-sufficient, most perfect god. Although he did make use of the relevant auxiliary causes, it was he himself who gave their fair design to all that comes to be. That is why we must distinguish two forms of cause, the divine and the necessary. First, the divine, for which

69   we must search in all things if we are to gain a life of happiness to the extent that our nature allows, and second, the necessary, for which we must search for the sake of the divine. Our reason is that without the necessary, those other objects, about which we are serious, cannot on their own be discerned, and hence cannot be comprehended or partaken of in any other way.

We have now sorted out the different kinds of cause, which lie ready for us like lumber for carpenters. From them we are to weave together the remainder of our account. So let us briefly return to our starting point and quickly proceed to the same place

b   from which we arrived at our present position.[81] Let us try to put

---

81. The starting point, as the immediate sequel makes clear, is the Craftsman's introduction of order and proportionality upon the precosmic "traces" of the

a final "head" on our account, one that fits in with our previous discussion.

To repeat what was said at the outset, the things we see were in a condition of disorderliness when the god introduced as much proportionality into them and in as many ways—making each thing proportional both to itself and to other things—as was possible for making them be commensurable and proportionate. For at the time they had no proportionality at all, except by chance, nor did any of them qualify at all for the names we now use to name them, names like *fire*, *water*, and so on. All these things, rather, the god first gave order to, and then out of them he pro-   c
ceeded to construct this universe, a single living thing that contains within itself all living things, mortal or immortal. He himself fashioned those that were divine, but assigned his own progeny the task of fashioning the generation of those that were mortal.

They imitated him: having taken the immortal origin of the soul, they proceeded next to encase it within a round mortal body [i.e., the head], and to give it the entire body as its vehicle. And within the body they built another kind of soul as well, the mortal kind, which contains within it those dreadful but necessary distur-   d
bances: pleasure, first of all, evil's most powerful lure; then pains, that make us run away from what is good; besides these, boldness also and fear, foolish counselors both; then also the spirit of anger hard to assuage, and expectation easily led astray. These they fused with unreasoning sense perception and all-venturing lust, and so, as was necessary, they constructed the mortal type of soul. In the face of these disturbances they scrupled to stain the divine soul only to the extent that this was absolutely necessary, and so they provided a home for the mortal soul in another place   e
in the body, away from the other, once they had built an isthmus as boundary between the head and the chest by situating a neck between them to keep them apart. Inside the chest, then, and in what is called the trunk, they proceeded to enclose the mortal type of soul. And since one part of the mortal soul was naturally superior to the other, they built the hollow of the trunk in sections, dividing them the way that women's quarters are divided from   70
men's. They situated the midriff between the sections to serve as a partition. Now the part of the mortal soul that exhibits manliness

---

elements. That activity is described at 31b–32c, and recalled as "beginning" at 48b–c. The "same place" is the account of the physics and physiology of perceptual properties and experiences just completed—an account now to be elaborated into a more general physiological and psychological account.

and spirit, the ambitious part, they settled nearer the head, between the midriff and the neck, so that it might listen to reason and together with it restrain by force the part consisting of appetites, should the latter at any time refuse outright to obey the
b dictates of reason coming down from the citadel. The heart, then, which ties the veins together, the spring from which blood courses with vigorous pulse throughout all the bodily members, they set in the guardhouse. That way, if spirit's might should boil over at a report from reason that some wrongful act involving these members is taking place—something being done to them from outside or even something originating from the appetites within—every bodily part that is sensitive may be keenly sensitized, through all the narrow vessels, to the exhortations or threats and so listen and follow completely. In this way the best part among them all can be left in charge.

c   The gods foreknew that the pounding of the heart (which occurs when one expects what one fears or when one's spirit is aroused) would, like all such swelling of the passions, be caused by fire. So they devised something to relieve the pounding: they implanted lungs, a structure that is first of all soft and without blood and that secondly contains pores bored through it like a
d sponge. This enables it to take in breath and drink and thereby cool the heart, bringing it respite and relaxation in the heat. That, then, is why they cut the passages of the windpipe down to the lungs and situated the lungs around the heart like padding, so that when spirit within the heart should reach its peak, the heart might pound against something that gives way to it and be cooled down. By laboring less, it might be better able to join spirit in serving reason.

The part of the soul that has appetites for food and drink and
e whatever else it feels a need for, given the body's nature, they settled in the area between the midriff and the boundary toward the navel. In the whole of this region they constructed something like a trough for the body's nourishment. Here they tied this part of the soul down like a beast, a wild one, but one they could not avoid sustaining along with the others if a mortal race were ever to be. They assigned it its position there, to keep it ever feeding at its trough, living as far away as possible from the part that takes counsel, and making as little clamor and noise as possible,
71 thereby letting the supreme part take its counsel in peace about what is beneficial for one and all. They knew that this part of the soul was not going to understand the deliverances of reason and

that even if it were in one way or another to have some awareness of them, it would not have an innate regard for any of them, but would be much more enticed by images and phantoms night and day. Hence the god conspired with this very tendency by constructing a liver, a structure which he situated in the dwelling   *b* place of this part of the soul. He made it into something dense, smooth, bright and sweet, though also having a bitter quality, so that the force of the thoughts sent down from the mind might be stamped upon it as upon a mirror that receives the stamps and returns visible images. So the force of the mind's thoughts could frighten this part of the soul whenever it could avail itself of a congenial portion of the liver's bitterness and threaten it with severe command. And by infusing the bitterness all over the liver, it could project bilious colors onto it and shrink the whole liver, making it wrinkled and rough. It could curve and shrivel up the   *c* liver's lobe and block up and close off its receptacles and portal fissures, thereby causing pains and bouts of nausea. And again, whenever thought's gentle inspiration should paint quite opposite pictures, its force would bring respite from the bitterness by refusing to stir up or to make contact with a nature opposite to its own. It would instead use the liver's own natural sweetness on it and restore the whole extent of it to be straight and smooth   *d* and free, and make that portion of the soul that inhabits the region around the liver gracious and well behaved, conducting itself with moderation during the night when, seeing that it has no share in reason and understanding, it practices divination by dreams. For our creators recalled their father's instruction to make the mortal race as excellent as possible, and so, redeeming even the base part of ourselves in this way, they set the center of   *e* divination here, so that it might have some grasp of truth.[82]

The claim that god gave divination as a gift to human folly has good support: while he is in his right mind no one engages in divination, however divinely inspired and true it may be, but only when his power of understanding is bound in sleep or by sickness, or when some sort of possession works a change in him. On the other hand, it takes a man who has his wits about him to recall and ponder the pronouncements produced by this state of divination or possession, whether in sleep or while awake. It takes

---

82. Traditionally, omens were read by "diviners" from the entrails, and especially the liver, of sacrificial animals. Timaeus, however, prefers to see the liver as the "seat" of divination through its function in dreams.

72   such a man to thoroughly analyze any and all visions that are
seen, to determine how and for whom they signify some future,
past, or present good or evil. But as long as the fit remains on
him, the man is incompetent to render judgment on his own
visions and voices; as the ancient proverb well puts it, "Only a
man of sound mind may know himself and conduct his own
b   affairs." This is the reason why it is customary practice to appoint
interpreters to render judgment on an inspired divination. These
persons are called "diviners" by some who are entirely ignorant
of the fact that they are expositors of utterances or visions communicated through riddles. Instead of "diviners," the correct thing
to call them is "interpreters of things divined."

This, then, explains why the liver's nature is what it is, and
why it is situated in the region we say—it is for the purpose of
divination. Now while each creature is still alive, an organ of this
sort will display marks that are fairly clear, but once its life has
c   gone, the organ turns blind and its divinations are too faint to
display any clear marks. Moreover, the neighboring organ situated on its left turns out to have a structure that is meant to serve
the liver in keeping it bright and clean continuously, like a dust
cloth provided for wiping a mirror, placed next to it and always
available. Hence, whenever impurities of one sort or another, the
effects of bodily illnesses, turn up all around the liver, the spleen,
a loosely woven organ with hollow spaces that contain no blood,
d   cleans them all away and absorbs them. In consequence it becomes
engorged with the impurities it has cleaned off, swells to great
size and festers. Later, when the body's cleansing is complete,
the swelling subsides, and the spleen once again shrinks to its
normal size.

So, as for our questions concerning the soul—to what extent
it is mortal and to what extent divine; where its parts are situated,
with what organs they are associated, and why they are situated
apart from one another—that the truth has been told is something
we could affirm only if we had divine confirmation. But that our
account is surely at least a "likely" one is a claim we must risk,
both now and as we proceed to examine the matter more closely.
Let that be our claim, then.

e   Our next topic must be pursued along the same lines. This
was to describe how the rest of the body came to be.[83] The follow-

---

83. Compare 61c: ". . . we have so far discussed neither the coming to be of flesh,
or of what pertains to flesh, nor the part of the soul that is mortal."

ing train of reasoning should explain its composition best of all. The creators of our race knew that we were going to be undisciplined in matters of food and drink. They knew that our gluttony would lead us to consume much more than the moderate amount we needed. So, to prevent the swift destruction of our mortal race by diseases and to forestall its immediate, premature demise, they had the foresight to create the lower abdomen, as it's called, as a receptacle for storing the excess food and drink. They wound the intestines round in coils to prevent the nourishment from passing through so quickly that the body would of necessity require fresh nourishment just as quickly, thereby rendering it insatiable. Such gluttony would make our whole race incapable of philosophy and the arts, and incapable of heeding the most divine part within us. 73

As for flesh and bones and things of that nature, this is how it is. The starting point for all these was the formation of marrow. For life's chains, as long as the soul remains bound to the body, are bound within the marrow, giving roots for the mortal race. The marrow itself came to be out of other things. For the god isolated from their respective kinds those primary triangles which were undistorted and smooth, and hence, owing to their exactness, were particularly well suited to make up fire, water, air, and earth. He mixed them together in the right proportions and from them made the marrow, a "universal seed" contrived for every mortal kind. Next, he implanted in the marrow the various types of soul and bound them fast in it. And in making his initial distribution, he proceeded immediately to divide the marrow into the number and kinds of shapes that matched the number and kinds of shapes that the types of soul were to possess, type by type. He then proceeded to mold the "field," as it were, that was to receive the divine seed, making it round, and called this portion of the marrow "brain." Each living thing was at its completion to have a head to function as a container for this marrow. That, however, which was to hold fast the remaining, mortal part of the soul, he divided into shapes that were at once round and elongated, all of which he named "marrow." And from these, as from anchors, he put out bonds to secure the whole soul, and so he proceeded to construct our bodies all around this marrow, beginning with the formation of solid bone as a covering for the whole of it. b

c

d

This is how he constructed bone. He sifted earth that was pure and smooth, kneaded it and soaked it with marrow. Next he set e this mixture in fire and then dipped it in water, then back in fire, followed by water again. By moving it this way repeatedly from the one and then back to the other, he made it insoluble by both. He made use of this material in shaping a round, bony globe to 74 enclose the brain, and left it with a narrow passage out. From the material he then proceeded to mold vertebrae to enclose marrow of the neck and back, and set them in place one underneath another, beginning with the head and proceeding along the whole length of the trunk, to function as pivots. And so, to preserve all of the seed, he fenced it in with a stony enclosure. In this enclosure he made joints, employing in their case the character of the Different situated between them to allow them to move and to flex.

b   Moreover, the god thought that bone as such was rather too brittle and inflexible, and also that repeatedly getting extremely hot and cold by turns would cause it to disintegrate and to destroy in short order the seed within it. That is why he contrived to make sinews and flesh. He bound all the limbs together with sinews that could contract and relax, and so enabled the body to flex about the pivots and to stretch itself out. The flesh he made as a defense against summer's heat and as protection against winter's cold. And, as protection against injuries, too, he made c the flesh so that it would give way softly and gently to bodies [impacting upon it], like the felted coverings we wear. He made it to contain within itself a warm moisture that would come out as perspiration during summertime, when, by moistening the body on the outside, it would impart the body's own coolness to the whole of it. And conversely, in wintertime this moisture would provide an adequate defense, by means of this fire[84] against the frost that surrounds it and attacks it from outside. Such were the designs of him who molded us like wax: he made a mixture using water, fire, and earth, which he adjusted together, and created a d compound of acid and brine, a fermented mixture that he combined with the previous mixture, and so he formed flesh, sappy and soft. The sinews he made out of a mixture of bone and unfermented flesh, to make up a single yellow stuff whose character was intermediate between them both. That is the reason the sinews came to have a stretchier and tougher character than flesh, yet softer and more moist than bone. With these the god wrapped

---

84. That is, the heat contained in the moisture.

the bones and the marrow. First he bound the bones to each other with sinews, and then he laid a shroud of flesh upon them all.   *e*

All those bones that had more soul than others he proceeded to wrap in a very thin layer of flesh, while those that contained less he wrapped in a very thick layer of very dense flesh. And indeed, at the joints of the bones, where it appeared that reason did not absolutely require the presence of flesh, he introduced only a thin layer of flesh, so that the ability of the joints to flex would not be impeded, a condition that would have made it very difficult for the bodies to move. A further reason was this: if there were a thick layer of flesh there, packed extremely densely together, its hardness would cause a kind of insensibility, which would make thinking less retentive and more obscure. This he wanted to prevent.

This explains why thighs and calves, the area around the hips,   *75* arms (both upper and lower), and all other bodily parts where there are no joints as well as all the internal bones, are all fully provided with flesh. It is because they have only small amounts of soul in their marrow, and so are devoid of intelligence. On the other hand, all those bodily parts that do possess intelligence are less fleshy, except perhaps for a fleshy thing—the tongue, for example—that was created to be itself an organ of sensation. But in most cases it is as I said. For there is no way that anything whose generation and composition are a consequence of Necessity   *b* can accommodate the combination of thick bone and massive flesh with keen and responsive sensation. If these two characteristics had not refused their concomitance, our heads above all else would have been so constituted as to possess this combination, and the human race, crowned with a head fortified with flesh and sinews, would have a life twice, or many more times, as long, a healthier and less painful life than the one we have now. As it was, however, our makers calculated the pros and cons of giving   *c* our race greater longevity but making it worse, versus making it better though less long-lived, and decided that the superior though shorter life span was in every way preferable for everyone to the longer but inferior one. This is why they capped the head with a sparse layer of bone—not with flesh and sinew, given that the head has no joints. For all these reasons, then, the head has turned out to be more sensitive and intelligent but also, in every man's case, much weaker than the body to which it is attached. With this in mind the god thus positioned sinews at the very   *d* edge of the head, around the neck, and welded them uniformly. To these sinews he fastened the ends of the jawbones underneath the face. The other sinews he shared out among all the limbs, fastening joint to joint.

e   Our makers fitted the mouth out with teeth, a tongue, and lips in their current arrangement, to accommodate both what is necessary and what is best: they designed the mouth as the entry passage for what is necessary and as the exit for what is best: for all that comes in and provides nourishment for the body is necessary, while that stream of speech that flows out through the mouth, that instrument of intelligence, is the fairest and best of all streams.

Moreover, the head couldn't be left to consist of nothing but bare bone, in view of the extremes of seasonal heat and cold. On the other hand, any mass of flesh with which it might be veiled couldn't be allowed to make it dull and insensitive, either. And 76   so, an outer layer, disproportionately large (the thing we now call "skin"), was separated off from the flesh [of the upper body] that wasn't drying out completely. The moisture in the area of the brain enabled this layer to draw together toward itself and grow so as to envelop the head all around. Coming up under the sutures, this moisture watered it, and closed it together upon the crown, drawing it together in a knot, as it were. The sutures varied considerably, owing to the effect of the revolutions [in the head][85] and of the nourishment taken: the greater the conflict *b*   among these revolutions, the more numerous the sutures—the lesser the conflict, the less numerous they were.

Now the divine part [the brain] began to puncture this whole area of skin all around with its fire. Once the skin was pierced and the moisture had exuded outward through it, all that was purely wet and hot went away. The part that was compounded of the same stuff that the skin was made up of, caught up by this motion, was stretched to a great length outside this skin, no thicker than the punctured hole [through which it passed]. However, it moved slowly, and so the surrounding air pushed it back inside *c*   to curl underneath the skin and take root there. This is the process by which hair has come to grow on the skin. Hair is something fibrous, made of the same stuff as the skin, though harder and more dense due to the felting effect of the cooling process: once a hair separates off from skin, it is cooled and so gets felted together.

---

85. Compare 43a *ff.*

With this stuff, then, our maker made our heads bushy, availing himself of the causal factors just described. His intention was that this, not bare flesh, ought to provide a protective covering for the part of the head that holds the brain: it was light, and *d* just right for providing shade in summer, and shelter in winter, without obstructing or interfering with the head's sensitivity in any way.

Sinew, skin, and bone were interwoven at the ends of our fingers and toes. The mixture of these three was dried out, resulting in the formation of a single stuff, a piece of hard skin, the same in every case. Now these were merely auxiliary causes in its formation—the preeminent cause of its production was the purpose that took account of future generations: our creators *e* understood that one day women and the whole realm of wild beasts would one day come to be from men, and in particular they knew that many of these offspring would need the use of nails and claws or hoofs for many purposes.[86] This is why they took care to include nails formed in a rudimentary way in their design for humankind, right at the start. This was their reason, then, and these the professed aims that guided them in making skin, hair, and nails grow at the extremities of our limbs.

So all the parts, all the limbs of the mortal living thing, came to constitute a natural whole. Of necessity, however, it came about 77 that he lived his life surrounded by fire and air, which caused him to waste away and be depleted, and so to perish. The gods, therefore, devised something to protect him. They made another mixture and caused another nature to grow, one congenial to our human nature though endowed with other features and other sensations, so as to be a different living thing. These are now cultivated trees, plants, and seeds, taught by the art of agriculture to be domesticated for our use. But at first there were only wild *b* kinds, older than our cultivated kinds. We may call these plants "living things" on the ground that anything that partakes of life has an incontestable right to be called a "living thing."[87] And in fact, what we are talking about now partakes of the third type of soul, the type that our account has situated between the midriff

---

86. See below, 90e–92c.

87. The word for living things here, *zōa*, (which is often appropriately translated "animals"), is cognate with Timaeus' word for "life." His point is that because plants have "life" (*zēn*), they are appropriately called *zōa*, even though they are not animals.

and the navel. This type is totally devoid of opinion, reasoning, or understanding, though it does share in sensation, pleasant and painful, and desires. For throughout its existence it is completely passive, and its formation has not entrusted it with a natural ability to discern and reflect upon any of its own characteristics, c by revolving within and about itself, repelling movement from without and exercising its own inherent movement. Hence it is alive, to be sure, and unmistakably a living thing, but it stays put, standing fixed and rooted, since it lacks self-motion.

All these varieties were planted by our masters, to whom we are subject, to nourish us. Having done that, they proceeded to cut channels throughout our bodies, like water pipes in a garden, so that our bodies could be irrigated, as it were, by an oncoming stream. First, they cut two blood veins, channels hidden under-
d neath the skin where the flesh joins it, to go down either side of the back, given that the body is a twofold thing, with a right and a left side. They situated these veins alongside the spine, and between them they placed the life-giving marrow as well, to give it its best chance to flourish, and to allow the bloodstream, which courses downhill, to flow readily from this region and uniformly irrigate the other parts of the body. They next split these veins
e in the region of the head and wove them through one another, crossing them in opposite directions. They diverted the veins from the right toward the left side of the body, and those from the left toward the right, so that they, together with the skin, would act as a bond to keep the head fastened to the body, seeing that there were no sinews attached to the crown to enclose the head all around. They did this especially to make sure that the stimulations received by the senses, coming from either side of the body, might register clearly upon the body as a whole.

From here the gods proceeded to fashion the irrigation system
78 in the following way. We'll come to see it more easily if we can first agree on this point: whatever is made up of smaller parts holds in larger parts, while whatever consists of larger parts is incapable of holding in smaller parts. Of all the elemental kinds, fire is made up of the smallest parts, and that is the reason it can pass through water, earth, and air, and any of their compounds. Nothing can hold it in. Now we must apply the same point to
b our belly. When food and drink descend into it, it holds them in, but it cannot hold in air and fire, consisting as they do of smaller parts than it does. And so the god availed himself of fire and air to conduct moisture from the belly to the [two] veins. He wove

together an interlaced structure of air and fire, something like a fish trap. At its entrance it had a pair of funnels, one of which in turn he subdivided into two. And from the funnels he stretched reeds, as it were, all around throughout the structure, right to its extremities. All the interior parts of this network he made of fire;   c
the funnels and the shell he made of air.

He took this structure and set it around the living thing that he had fashioned, in the following way. The funnel part he inserted into the mouth, and, consisting as it did of two funnels, he let one of them descend into the lungs down the windpipe, and the other alongside the windpipe into the belly. He made a split in the first one and assigned each of its parts a common outlet by way of the nostrils, so that when the one part fails to provide passage by way of the mouth, all of its currents also   d
might be replenished from that one [i.e., by way of the nostrils]. The shell, the other part of the trap, he made to grow around the hollow part of the body, and he made this whole thing now flow together onto the funnels [compressing them]—gently, because they are made of air—and now, when the funnels flow back [expanding again], he made the interlaced structure sink into and through the body, a relatively porous thing, and pass outside again.[88] The interior rays of fire [inside the shell], bound from side to side, he made to follow the air as it passed in both directions. This process was to go on nonstop for as long as the mortal   e
living thing holds together; and this, of course, is the phenomenon to which the name-giver (so we claim) assigned the names of *inhalation* and *exhalation*. This entire pattern of action and reaction, irrigating and cooling our bodies, supports their nutrition and life. For whenever the internal fire, united with the breath that passes in or out, follows it along, it surges up and down continually and makes its way through and into the belly, where it gets   79
hold of the food and drink. These it dissolves or breaks up into tiny parts, which it then takes through the outbound passages along which it is advancing, and transfers them into the [two] veins, as water from a spring is transferred into water pipes. And so it causes the currents of the veins to flow through the body as through a conduit.

---

88. As 79c–e seems to show, Timaeus appears to envisage the "shell" as an envelope of air surrounding the exterior of the torso, being drawn through the interstices of the body into the interior and then pushed out again, as breathing takes place.

Let us, however, take another look at what happens in respiration. What explains its having the character that it now actually
b has? It is this. Since there is no void into which anything that is moving could enter, and since the air we breathe out does move out, away from us, it clearly follows that this air doesn't move into a void, but pushes the air next to it out of its place. As this air is pushed out, it drives out the air next to it, and so on, and so inevitably the air, displaced all around, enters the place from which the original air was breathed out and refills that place,
c following hard on the breath. This all takes place at once, like the rotation of a wheel, because there is no such thing as a void. Consequently even as the breath is being discharged, the area of the chest and the lungs fills up again with the air that surrounds the body, air that goes through the cycle of displacement and penetrates the porous flesh. And again, when the air is turned back and passes outward through the body, it comes round to push respiration inward by way of the mouth and the nostrils.

How did these processes get started? The explanation, we
d must suppose, is this: in the case of every living thing, its inner parts that are close to the blood and the veins are its hottest parts—an inner spring of fire inside it, as it were. This, of course, is what we've been comparing to the interlaced structure of a fish trap; it is entirely woven of fire, we said, and extended throughout its middle, while the rest of it, the external parts, are woven of air. Now it is beyond dispute that what is hot has a natural tendency to move outward into its own proper region, toward that which is akin to it. In this case there are two passages out,
e one out through [the pores of] the body, and the other out through the mouth and nose. So whenever hot air rushes out the one passage, it pushes air around into the other, and the air so pushed around gets hot as it encounters the fire, while the air that passes out is cooled down. Now as the temperature changes and the air that enters by way of one or the other of the passages gets hotter, the hotter air is more inclined to return by way of the passage it entered, since it moves toward what is like itself, and so it pushes air around to and through the other passage. This air is affected the same way, and produces the same effect every time; and so, due to both these principles it produces an oscillation back and forth, thereby providing for inhalation and exhalation to occur.

In this connection we should pursue along these lines an in-
80 quiry into the causes of the phenomena associated with medical cupping, and of swallowing, as well as of the motion of all projec-

tiles that are dispatched into the air and along the ground. We should also investigate all sounds, whether fast or slow—sounds that appear to us as high-pitched or low. Sometimes, when the motion they produce in us as they move toward us lacks conformity, these sounds are inharmonious; at other times, when the motion does have conformity, the sounds are harmonious. [What happens in the latter case is this.] The slower sounds catch up with the motions of the earlier and quicker sounds as these are already dying away and have come to a point of conformity with *b* the motions produced by the slower sounds that travel later. In catching up with them, the slower sounds do not upset them, even though they introduce another motion. On the contrary, they graft onto the quicker movement, now dying away, the beginning of a slower one that conforms to it, and so they produce a single effect, a mixture of high and low. Hence the pleasure they bring to fools and the delight they afford—by their expression of divine harmony in mortal movement—to the wise.

And what is more, every kind of water current, even the *c* descent of a thunderbolt as well as that marvelous "attraction" exercised by amber and by the lodestone, in all these cases there is no such thing as a force of attraction. As any careful investigator will discover, there is no void; these things push themselves around into each other; all things move by exchanging places, each to its own place, whether in the process of combination or of dissolution. He will discover that these "works of wizardry" are due to the interactive relationships among these phenomena.

The phenomenon of respiration, which provided the occasion *d* for this account, is a case in point. The above are the principles and causes to which it owes its existence, as we have said before. The fire cuts up the food [in our bellies] and as it follows the breath it oscillates inside us. As the oscillation goes on, the fire pumps the cut-up bits of food from the belly and packs them into the veins. This is the mechanism by which the streams of nourishment continue to flow throughout the bodies of all living things. The bits of food, freshly cut up and derived from things like themselves—from fruits or from vegetables which the god *e* had caused to grow for this very purpose, to serve us as food— come to have a variety of colors as a result of being mixed together, but a reddish color pervading them predominates, a character that is the product of the cutting and staining action of fire upon moisture. This is why the color of the liquid that flows in our bodies looks the way we've described; this liquid we call *blood*,

81   which feeds our flesh and indeed our whole bodies. From this
     source the various parts of our bodies are watered and so replen-
     ish the supports of the depleted areas. Now both processes, the
     replenishment and the depletion, follow the manner of the move-
     ment of anything within the universe at large: everything moves
     toward that which is of its own kind. In this case, our external
     environment continually wastes us away and distributes our bulk
     by dispatching each [elemental] kind toward its own sort. The
     ingredients in our blood, then, having been chopped up inside
b   us and encompassed by the individual living thing as by the
     frame of the heavens, of necessity imitate the universe's motion.
     And so, as each of the fragmented parts inside moves toward its
     own kind, it replenishes once again the area just then depleted.
     In every case, whenever there is more leaving a body than flowing
     in [to replenish it], it diminishes; whenever less, the body grows.
     So while a living thing's constitution is still young, and its elemen-
     tal triangles are "fresh from the slips," as it were, the triangles
     are firmly locked together, even though the frame of its entire
c   mass is pliable, seeing that it has just lately been formed from
     marrow and nourished with milk. Now when the triangles that
     constitute the young living thing's food and drink enter its body
     from the outside and are enveloped within it, the body's own
     new triangles cut and prevail over these others, which are older
     and weaker than they are. The living thing is thus nourished by
     an abundance of like parts, and so made to grow big. But when
     the roots of the triangles are slackened as a result of numerous
     conflicts they have waged against numerous adversaries over a
d   long period of time, they are no longer able to cut up the entering
     food-triangles into conformity with themselves. They are them-
     selves handily destroyed by the invaders from outside. Every
     living thing, then, goes into decline when it loses this battle, and
     it suffers what we call "old age." Eventually the interlocking
     bonds of the triangles around the marrow can no longer hold on,
     and come apart under stress, and when this happens they let the
     bonds of the soul go. The soul is then released in a natural way,
e   and finds it pleasant to take its flight. All that is unnatural, we
     recall, is painful, while all that occurs naturally is pleasant. This
     is true of death as well: a death that is due to disease or injury
     is painful and forced, while a death that comes naturally, when
     the aging process has run its course, is of all deaths the least
     distressing—a pleasant, not a painful death.

82   How diseases originate is, I take it, obvious to all. Given that

there are four kinds of stuff out of which the body has been constructed—earth, fire, water, and air—it may happen that some of these unnaturally increase themselves at the expense of the others. Or they may switch regions, each leaving its own and moving into another's region. Or again, since there is in fact more than one variety of fire and the other stuffs, it may happen that a given bodily part accommodates a particular variety that is not appropriate for it. When these things happen, they bring on conflicts and diseases. For when any of these unnatural occurrences and changes take place, bodily parts that used to be cold become hot, or those that are dry go on to become moist, and so   *b* with light and heavy, too. They undergo all sorts of changes in all sorts of ways. Indeed, it is our view that only when that which arrives at or leaves a particular bodily part is the same as that part, consistent, uniform, and in proper proportion with it, will the body be allowed to remain stable, sound, and healthy. On the other hand, anything that causes offense by passing beyond these bounds as it arrives or departs will bring on a multiplicity of altered states, and an infinity of diseases and degenerations.

Furthermore, since there is a class of secondary structures to be found in nature, anyone who intends to understand diseases   *c* will have a second set of subjects to study. Since marrow and bone, flesh and sinew are composed of the elemental stuffs— from which blood also has been formed, though in a different way—most of the diseases are brought on in the manner just described. But the most serious and grievous diseases are contracted when the process of generation that led to the formation of these structures is reversed. When this happens, they degenerate. It is natural for flesh and sinews to be formed from blood, the sinew from the fiber (which is of its own kind) and the flesh   *d* from the part of the blood that congeals when the sinew is separated from it. And the sticky and oily stuff that in its turn emerges from the sinew and the flesh both glues the flesh to the bone and feeds the marrow-encompassing bone itself, so causing it to grow. And because the bone is so dense, the part of this stuff that filters through, consisting as it does of the purest, smoothest, and oiliest kinds of triangles, forms droplets inside the bone and waters the   *e* marrow. And when this is the way it actually happens in each case, health will generally result.

Disease, however, will result if things happen the other way around. For when flesh that is wasting away passes its waste back into the veins, the veins will contain not only air but also

an excess of blood of great variety. This blood will have a multitude of colors and bitter aspects, and even acidic and salty qualities, and will contain bile and serum and phlegm of every sort. These are all back-products and agents of destruction. To begin
83   with, they corrupt the blood itself, and then also they do not supply the body any further with nourishment. They move everywhere throughout the veins, no longer keeping to the order of natural circulation. They are hostile to one another, since none receives any advantage from any other, and they wage a destructive and devastating war against the constituents of the body that have stayed intact and kept to their posts.

Now as the oldest part of the flesh wastes away, it resists assimilation. It turns black as a result of being subjected to a prolonged process of burning, and because it is thoroughly eaten
b   up it is bitter, and so it launches a severe attack against any part of the body that has not yet been destroyed. Sometimes the bitterness is largely refined away, and then the black color acquires an acidic quality that replaces the bitter. At other times, though, the bitterness is steeped in blood, and then it comes to have more of a reddish color, and when the black is mixed with this, it becomes a grass-like green. Further, when the flesh that is disintegrated by the fire of the inflammation is fairly young, the color that is mixed with the bitterness is a yellowish orange. Now the name "bile," common to all these varieties, was given
c   to them either by doctors, possibly, or else by someone who had the ability to look at a plurality of unlike things and see in them a single kind that deserves to be called by a single name. As for everything that can be called a variety of bile, each has its own distinctive definition, depending on its color. In the case of serum, some of it, the watery part of the blood, is benign, while that which is a part of the black, acid bile is malignant when heat causes it to be mixed with a salty quality. This kind of thing is called acid phlegm. Furthermore, when the stuff that comes from
d   the disintegration of young, tender flesh is exposed to air and blown up with wind and enveloped in moisture, bubbles form as a result, each one too small to be seen though collectively amounting to a visible mass. These bubbles look white, as foam begins to form. All this disintegration of tender flesh reacting with air is what we call white phlegm. Newly formed phlegm, furthermore, has a watery part that consists of perspiration and
e   tears, as well as any other impurities that are discharged every day. So whenever the blood, instead of being replenished in the

natural way by nutrients from food and drink, derives its volume from opposite sources, contrary to nature's way, all these things, it turns out, serve as instruments of disease.

Now when a certain part of the flesh is decomposed by disease, as long as the foundations of the flesh remain intact, the effect of the calamity is only half of what it would otherwise be, for there is still a chance of an easy recovery. But when the stuff that binds *84* the flesh to the bones becomes diseased and no longer nourishes the bone or binds the flesh to the bone because it is now separated from flesh and bone as well as from sinews,[89] it turns from being slick and smooth and oily to being rough and briny, shriveled up in consequence of its bad regimen. When this occurs, all the stuff that this happens to crumbles away back into the flesh and the sinew, and separates from the bone. The flesh, which collapses with it away from its roots, leaves the sinews bare and full of *b* brine. And the flesh itself succumbs back into the bloodstream, where it works to aggravate the previously mentioned diseases.

Severe as these bodily processes are, those disorders that affect the more basic tissues are even more serious. When the density of the flesh prevents the bone from getting enough ventilation, the bone gets moldy, which causes it to get too hot. Gangrene sets in and the bone cannot take in its nourishment. It then crum- *c* bles and, by a reverse process, is dissolved into that nourishment which, in its turn, enters the flesh, and as the flesh lands in the blood it causes all of the previously mentioned diseases to become more virulent still. But the most extreme case of all is when the marrow becomes diseased, either as a result of some deficiency or some excess. This produces the most serious, the most critically fatal diseases, in which all the bodily processes are made to flow backward.

Further, there is a third class of diseases, which we should think of as arising in three ways: *d*

(1) One way is from air that we breathe;
(2) another from phlegm; and
(3) the third from bile.

(1) When the lungs, the dispensers of air to the body, are obstructed by humors, they do not permit a clear passage. At some places the air cannot get in, while at others more than the

---

89. Reading *au to ex ekeinōn hama kai neurōn* at a2.

appropriate amount gets in. In the former case, there will be parts of the body that don't get any breath and so begin to decay, while in the latter case the air forces its way through the veins and twists them together like strands. It makes its way into the central region of the body, the region that contains the midriff, where it
e is shut in, thereby causing the body to waste away. These factors produce countless painful diseases, often accompanied by profuse perspiration. And often, when flesh disintegrates inside the body, air is produced there but is unable to get out. This air then causes just as much excruciating pain as the air that comes in from outside. The pain is most severe when the air settles around the sinews and the veins there and causes them to swell, thereby stretching backward the "back stays" (the great sinews of the shoulder and arm) and the sinews attached to them. It is from this phenomenon of stretching, of course, that the diseases called *tetanus* ("tension") and *opisthotonus* ("backward stretching") have received their names. These diseases are difficult to cure. In fact,
85 the onset of a fever affords the best prospects for relief from such ailments.

(2) Now as for the white phlegm, as long as it is trapped [in the body], it is troublesome because of the air in its bubbles. But if it finds a vent to the outside of the body, it is gentler, even though it does deck the body with white, leprous spots and engenders the corresponding diseases. If it is mixed with black bile and the mixture is sprayed against the divine circuits in the head, thereby throwing them into confusion, the effect is fairly mild if it comes
b during sleep, but should it come upon someone while awake, it is much harder to shake off. Seeing that it is a disease of the sacred part of our constitution, it is entirely just that it should be called the "sacred" disease.[90]

Acid and salty phlegm is the source of all those diseases that come about by passage of fluids. These disorders have been given all sorts of different names, given that the bodily regions into which the fluids flow are quite diverse.

(3) All inflammations in the body (so called from their being burned or "set aflame") are caused by bile. When bile finds a
c vent to the outside, it boils over and sends up all sorts of tumors, but when it is shut up inside, it creates many inflammatory diseases. The worst occurs when the bile gets mixed with clean blood and disrupts the disposition of the blood's fibers, which

---

90. That is, epilepsy.

are interspersed throughout the blood. These fibers act to preserve a balance of thinness and thickness, that is, to prevent both the blood from getting so liquid, due to the body's heat, that it oozes out from the body's pores, and, on the other hand, its getting so dense that it is sluggish and hardly able to circulate within the *d* veins. The fibers, then, by virtue of their natural composition, preserve the appropriate state between these conditions. And even after death, when the blood cools down, if the fibers are [extracted from the blood] and collected, the residue will still be completely runny, while if they are left in the blood, they, along with the surrounding cold, congeal it in no time. Given, then, that the fibers have this effect upon the blood, though the bile— which originated as primitive blood and then from flesh was dissolved into blood again—is hot and liquid at first as a little of it invades the blood, it congeals under the effect of the fibers, and *e* as it congeals and is forced to extinguish its heat it causes internal cold and shivering. But as more of it flows in, it overpowers the fibers with its own heat. It boils over and shakes them up into utter confusion. And if it proves capable of sustaining its power to the end, it penetrates to the marrow and burns it up, thereby loosening the cables that hold the soul there, like a ship, and setting the soul free. But when there is rather little of it and the body resists its dissolution, the bile is itself overpowered and is expelled either by way of the body as a whole or else it is compressed through the veins into the lower or upper belly, and is expelled from the body like an exile from a city in civil strife, so *86* bringing on diarrhea, dysentery, and every disease of that kind. Bodies afflicted mostly by an excess of fire will generate continuous states of heat and fevers; those suffering from an excess of air produce fevers that recur every day; while those that have an excess of water have fevers that recur only every other day, given that water is more sluggish than air or fire. Bodies afflicted by an excess of earth, the most sluggish of the four, are purged within a fourfold cycle of time and produce fevers that occur every fourth day, fevers that are hard to get over.

The foregoing described how diseases of the body happen to *b* come about. The diseases of the soul that result from a bodily condition come about in the following way. It must be granted, surely, that mindlessness is the disease of the soul, and of mindlessness there are two kinds. One is madness, and the other is ignorance. And so if a man suffers from a condition that brings on either one or the other, that condition must be declared a disease.

We must lay it down that the diseases that pose the gravest dangers for the soul are excessive pleasures and pains. When a
c man enjoys himself too much or, in the opposite case, when he suffers great pain, and he exerts himself to seize the one and avoid the other in inopportune ways, he lacks the ability to see or hear anything right. He goes raving mad and is at that moment least capable of rational thought. And if the seed of a man's marrow grows to overflowing abundance like a tree that bears an inordinately plentiful quantity of fruit, he is in for a long series of bursts of pain, or of pleasures, in the area of his desires and their fruition. These severe pleasures and pains drive him mad
d for the greater part of his life, and though his body has made his soul diseased and witless, people will think of him not as sick, but as willfully bad. But the truth about sexual overindulgence is that it is a disease of the soul caused primarily by the condition of a single stuff which, due to the porousness of the bones, flows within the body and renders it moist. And indeed, just about every type of succumbing to pleasure is talked about as something reproachable, as though the bad things are willfully done. But it
e is not right to reproach people for them, for no one is willfully bad. A man becomes bad, rather, as a result of one or another corrupt condition of his body and an uneducated upbringing. No one who incurs these pernicious conditions would will to have them.

And as for pains, once again it is the body that causes the soul so much trouble, and in the same ways. When any of a man's acid and briny phlegms or any bitter and bilious humors wander up and down his body without finding a vent to the outside and
87 remain pent up inside, they mix the vapor that they give off with the motion of the soul and so are confounded with it. So they produce all sorts of diseases of the soul, some more intense and some more frequent than others. And as they move to the three regions of the soul, each of them produces a multitude of varieties of bad temper and melancholy in the region it attacks, as well as of recklessness and cowardice, not to mention forgetfulness and
b stupidity. Furthermore, when men whose constitutions are bad in this way have bad forms of government where bad civic speeches are given, both in public and in private, and where, besides, no studies that could remedy this situation are at all pursued by people from their youth on up, that is how all of us who are bad come to be that way—the products of two causes both entirely beyond our control. It is the begetters far more than

the begotten, and the nurturers far more than the nurtured, that bear the blame for all this. Even so, one should make every possible effort to flee from badness, whether with the help of one's upbringing or the pursuits or studies one undertakes, and to seize its opposite. But that is the subject for another speech.

The counterpart to the subject just dealt with, that is, how to   c
treat our bodies and states of mind and preserve them whole, is one that it is now fitting and right to give its turn. After all, good things have more of a claim to be the subject of our speech than bad things. Now all that is good is beautiful, and what is beautiful is not ill-proportioned. Hence we must take it that if a living thing is to be in good condition, it will be well-proportioned. We can perceive the less important proportions and do some figuring about them, but the more important proportions, which are of the greatest consequence, we are unable to figure out. In determining   d
health and disease or virtue and vice no proportion or lack of it is more important than that between soul and body—yet we do not think about any of them nor do we realize that when a vigorous and excellent soul is carried about by a too frail and puny frame, or when the two are combined in the opposite way, the living thing as a whole lacks beauty, because it is lacking in the most important of proportions. That living thing, however, which finds itself in the opposite condition [i.e., one that is well-proportioned] is, for those who are able to observe it, the most beautiful, the most desirable of all things to behold. Imagine a   e
body that lacks proportion because its legs are too long or something else is too big. It is not only ugly but also causes itself no end of troubles. As its parts try to cooperate to get its tasks done, it frequently tires itself out or gets convulsive, or, because it lurches this way and that, it keeps falling down. That's how we ought to think of that combination of soul and body which we call the Living Thing. When within it there is a soul more powerful than the body and this soul gets excited, it churns the whole being   88
and fills it from inside with diseases, and when it concentrates on one or another course of study or inquiry, it wears the body out. And again, when the soul engages in public or private teaching sessions or verbal battles, the disputes and contentions that then occur cause the soul to fire the body up and rock it back and forth, so inducing discharges that trick most so-called doctors into making misguided diagnoses. But when, on the other hand, a large body, too much for its soul, is joined with a puny and feeble mind, then, given that human beings have two sets of   b

natural desires—desires of the body for food and desires of the most divine part of us for wisdom—the motions of the stronger part will predominate, and amplify their own interest. They render the functions of the soul dull, stupid, and forgetful, thereby bringing on the gravest disease of all: ignorance.

From both of these conditions there is in fact one way to preserve oneself, and that is not to exercise the soul without exercising the body, nor the body without the soul, so that each

c may be balanced by the other and so be sound. The mathematician, then, or the ardent devotee of any other intellectual discipline, should also provide exercise for his body by taking part in gymnastics, while one who takes care to develop his body should in his turn practice the exercises of the soul by applying himself to the arts and to every pursuit of wisdom, if he is to truly deserve the joint epithets of "fine and good." And the various bodily parts

d should also be looked after in this same way, in imitation of the structure of the universe. For since the body is heated and cooled inside by things that enter it and is dried and moistened by things outside of it and made to undergo the consequent changes by both of these motions, it will happen that when a man subjects his body to these motions when it has been in a state of rest, the body is overcome and brought to ruin. But if he models himself after what we have called the foster mother and nurse of the universe and persistently refuses to allow his body any degree of rest but exercises and continually agitates it through its whole

e extent, he will keep in a state of natural equilibrium the internal and the external motions. And if the agitation is a measured one, he will succeed in bringing order and regularity to those disturbances and those [elemental] parts that wander all over the body according to their affinities in the way described in the account we gave earlier about the universe. He will not allow one hostile element to position itself next to another and so breed wars and diseases in the body. Instead, he will have one friendly

89 element placed by another, and so bring about health.

Now the best of the motions is one that occurs within oneself and is caused by oneself. This is the motion that bears the greatest kinship to understanding and to the motion of the universe. Motion that is caused by the agency of something else is less good. Worst of all is the motion that moves, part by part, a passive body in a state of rest, and does so by means of other things. That, then, is why the motion induced by physical exercise is the best of those that purify and restore the body. Second is that induced by the rocking motion of sea travel or travel in any other kind of conveyance that doesn't tire one out. The third type of *b* motion is useful in an occasional instance of dire need; barring that, however, no man in his right mind should tolerate it. This is medical purging by means of drugs. We should avoid aggravating with drugs diseases that aren't particularly dangerous. Every disease has a certain makeup that in a way resembles the natural makeup of living things. In fact, the constitution of such beings goes through an ordered series of stages throughout their life. This is true of the species as a whole, and also of its individual members, each of which is born with its allotted span of life, barring unavoidable accidents. This is because its triangles are so *c* made up, right from the beginning, as to have the capacity to hold up for a limited time beyond which life cannot be prolonged any further. Now diseases have a similar makeup, so that when you try to wipe them out with drugs before they have run their due course, the mild diseases are liable to get severe, and the occasional ones frequent. That is why you need to cater to all such diseases by taking care of yourself to the extent that you are free and have the time to do that. What you should not do *d* is aggravate a stubborn irritation with drugs.

Let these remarks suffice, then, on the subject of the living thing as a whole and its bodily parts, and how a man should both lead and be led by himself in order to have the best prospects for leading a rational life. Indeed, we must give an even higher priority to doing our utmost to make sure that the part that is to do the leading is as superbly and as perfectly as possible fitted for that task. Now a thoroughgoing discussion of these matters *e* would in and of itself be a considerable task, but if we treat it as a side issue, in line with what we have said before, it may not be out of turn to conclude our discourse with the following observations.

There are, as we have said many times now, three distinct types of soul that reside within us, each with its own motions. So now too, we must say in the same vein, as briefly as we can, that any type which is idle and keeps its motions inactive cannot but become very weak, while one that keeps exercising becomes very strong. And so we must keep watch to make sure that their *90* motions remain proportionate to each other.

Now we ought to think of the most sovereign part of our soul as god's gift to us, given to be our guiding spirit. This, of course, is the type of soul that, as we maintain, resides in the top part of

our bodies. It raises us up away from the earth and toward what
is akin to us in heaven, as though we are plants grown not from
the earth but from heaven. In saying this, we speak absolutely
correctly. For it is from heaven, the place from which our souls
were originally born, that the divine part suspends our head, that
b is, our root, and so keeps our whole body erect. So if a man has
become absorbed in his appetites or his ambitions and takes great
pains to further them, all his thoughts are bound to become merely
mortal. And so far as it is at all possible for a man to become
thoroughly mortal, he cannot help but fully succeed in this, seeing
that he has cultivated his mortality all along. On the other hand,
if a man has seriously devoted himself to the love of learning
and to true wisdom, if he has exercised these aspects of himself
c above all, then there is absolutely no way that his thoughts can
fail to be immortal and divine, should truth come within his
grasp. And to the extent that human nature can partake of immortality, he can in no way fail to achieve this: constantly caring for
his divine part as he does, keeping well-ordered the guiding spirit
that lives within him, he must indeed be supremely happy. Now
there is but one way to care for anything, and that is to provide
for it the nourishment and the motions that are proper to it. And
the motions that have an affinity to the divine part within us are
d the thoughts and revolutions of the universe. These, surely, are
the ones that each of us should follow. We should redirect the
revolutions in our heads that were thrown off course at our birth,[91]
by coming to learn the harmonies and revolutions of the universe,
and so bring into conformity with its objects our faculty of understanding, as it was in its original condition. And when this conformity is complete, we shall have achieved our goal: that most
excellent life offered to humankind by the gods, both now and forevermore.

e   And now indeed, it seems, we have all but completed our
initial assignment, that of tracing the history of the universe down
to the emergence of humankind. We should go on to mention
briefly how the other living things came to be—a topic that won't
require many words. By doing this we'll seem to be in better
measure with ourselves so far as our words on these subjects
are concerned.

        Let us proceed, then, to a discussion of this subject in the
following way. According to our likely account, all male-born

---

91. See 43a–44a.

humans who lived lives of cowardice or injustice were reborn in the second generation as women. And this explains why at that 91 time the gods fashioned the desire for sexual union, by constructing one ensouled living thing in us as well as another one in women. This is how they made them in each case: There is [in a man] a passage by which fluids exit from the body, where it receives the liquid that has passed through the lungs down into the kidneys and on into the bladder and expels it under pressure of air. From this passage they bored a connecting one into the compacted marrow that runs from the head along the neck through the spine. This is in fact the marrow that we have pre- b viously called "seed."[92] Now because it has soul in it and had now found a vent [to the outside], this marrow instilled a life-giving desire for emission right at the place of venting, and so produced the love of procreation. This is why, of course, the male genitals are unruly and self-willed, like an animal that will not be subject to reason and, driven crazy by its desires, seeks to overpower everything else. The very same causes operate in women. A woman's womb or uterus, as it is called, is a living c thing within her with a desire for childbearing. Now when this remains unfruitful for an unseasonably long period of time, it is extremely frustrated and travels everywhere up and down her body. It blocks up her respiratory passages, and by not allowing her to breathe it throws her into extreme emergencies, and visits all sorts of other illnesses upon her until finally the woman's desire and the man's love bring them together, and, like plucking d the fruit from a tree, they sow the seed into the ploughed field of her womb, living things too small to be visible and still without form. And when they have again given them distinct form, they nourish these living things so that they can mature inside the womb. Afterward, they bring them to birth, introducing them into the light of day.

That is how women and females in general came to be. As for birds, as a kind they are the products of a transformation. They grow feathers instead of hair. They descended from innocent but simpleminded men, men who studied the heavenly bodies but in their naiveté believed that the most reliable proofs concern- e ing them could be based upon visual observation. Land animals in the wild, moreover, came from men who had no tincture of philosophy and who made no study of the heavens whatsoever,

---

92. At 73c1; 74a4.

because they no longer made use of the revolutions in their heads but instead followed the lead of the parts of the soul that reside in the chest. As a consequence of these ways of theirs they carried their forelimbs and their heads dragging toward the ground, like toward like. The tops of their heads became elongated and took

92   all sorts of shapes, depending on the particular way in which the revolutions were squeezed together from lack of use. This is the reason animals of this kind have four or more feet. The god placed a greater number of supports under the more mindless beings so that they might be drawn more closely to the ground. As for the most mindless of these animals, the ones whose entire bodies stretch out completely along the ground, the gods made them without feet, crawling along the ground, there being no need of

b   feet anymore. The fourth kind of animal, the kind that lives in water, came from those men who were without question the most stupid and ignorant of all. The gods who brought about their transformation concluded that these no longer deserved to breathe pure air, because their souls were tainted with transgressions of every sort. Instead of letting them breathe rare and pure air, they shoved them into water to breathe its murky depths. This is the origin of fish, of all shellfish, and of every water-inhabiting animal. Their justly due reward for their extreme

c   stupidity is their extreme dwelling place. These, then, are the conditions that govern, both then and now, how all the animals exchange their forms, one for the other, and in the process lose or gain intelligence or folly.

And so now we may say that our account of the universe has reached its conclusion. This world of ours has received and teems with living things, mortal and immortal. A visible living thing containing visible ones, a perceptible god, image of the intelligible Living Thing,[93] its grandness, goodness, beauty, and perfection are unexcelled. Our one heaven, indeed the only one of its kind, has come to be.

---

93. Compare 30c–d and 39e.

SELECT BIBLIOGRAPHY

Books and Collections of Articles:

[1] Allen, R. E. (ed.), *Studies in Plato's Metaphysics*. London: Routledge & Kegan Paul, 1965.

[2] Anton, J. P., and G. Kustas (eds.), *Essays in Ancient Greek Philosophy*, vol. 1. Albany: SUNY Press, 1971.

[3] Anton, J. P., and A. Preus (eds.), *Essays in Ancient Greek Philosophy*, vol. 3: Plato. Albany: SUNY Press, 1989.

[4] Archer-Hind, R. D. (ed. and tr.), *The Timaeus of Plato*. London: McMillan & Co., 1888; repr. Salem, N.H.: Ayer Co. Publishers.

[5] Brandwood, L., *The Chronology of Plato's Dialogues*. Cambridge: Cambridge University Press, 1990.

[6] Brisson, L., *"Le Même et l'Autre dans la Structure Ontologique du Timée de Platon."* Sankt Augustin: Academia Verlag, 1994.

[7] ———, and F. Walter Meyerstein, *Inventer l'Univers*, Paris, 1991. English translation *Inventing the Universe*. Albany: SUNY Press, 1995.

[8] Calcidius, *Timaeus a Calcidio Translatus Commentarioque Instructus*, edited by J. H. Waszink. Leiden: Brill, 1962.

[9] Calvo, T., and L. Brisson (eds.), *Interpreting the* Timaeus *and* Critias. Sankt Augustin: Academia Verlag, 1997.

[10] Cherniss, H. F., *Selected Papers*, edited by L. Tarán. Leiden: Brill, 1977.

[11] ———, *Aristotle's Criticism of Plato and the Academy*. Baltimore: Johns Hopkins University Press, 1944; repr. New York: Russell and Russell, 1962.

[12] Cleary, J. (ed.), *Proceedings of the Boston Area Colloquium in Ancient Philosophy* 2. Lanham, Md.: University Press of America, 1986.

[13] Cooper, J. M., and D. S. Hutchinson (eds.), *Plato: Complete Works*. Indianapolis: Hackett Publishing Co., 1997.

[14] Cornford, F. M., *Plato's Cosmology*. London: Routledge & Kegan Paul, 1937; repr. Indianapolis: Hackett Publishing Co., 1997.

[15] DeVogel, C. J., *Philosophia I: Studies in Greek Philosophy*. Assen: Van Gorcum, 1970.

[16] ———, *Rethinking Plato and Platonism*. Leiden: Brill, 1986.

[17] Dicks, D. R., *Early Greek Astronomy*. Ithaca, N.Y.: Cornell University Press, 1970.

[18] Everson, S. (ed.), *Companions to Ancient Thought 3: Philosophy of Language*. Cambridge: Cambridge University Press, 1994.

[19] Frede, M., *Essays in Ancient Philosophy*. Minneapolis: Minnesota University Press, 1987.

[20] ——, *Prädikation und Existenzaussage, Hypomnemata 18*, Göttingen, 1976.

[21] —— and G. Striker (eds.), *Rationality in Greek Thought*. Oxford: Clarendon Press, 1996.

[22] Gill, C., and M. M. McCabe (eds.), *Form and Argument in Late Plato*. Oxford: Clarendon Press, 1996.

[23] Hampton, C., *Pleasure, Knowledge and Being*. Albany: SUNY Press, 1990.

[24] Kahn, C., *The Verb "Be" in Ancient Greek*. Dordrecht: Reidel, 1973.

[25] Kraut, R. (ed.), *Plato's Republic: Critical Essays*. Lanham, Md.: Rowman and Littlefield, 1997.

[26] —— (ed.), *The Cambridge Companion to Plato*. Cambridge: Cambridge University Press, 1992.

[27] Menn, S., *Plato on God as Nous*. Carbondale: Southern Illinois University Press, 1995.

[28] Mohr, R., *The Platonic Cosmology*. Leiden: Brill, 1985.

[29] Owen, G. E. L., *Logic, Science and Dialectic*, edited by M. Nussbaum. Ithaca, N.Y.: Cornell University Press, 1986.

[30] Patterson, R., *Image and Reality in Plato's Metaphysics*. Indianapolis: Hackett Publishing Co., 1985.

[31] Pelikan, J., *What Has Athens to Do with Jerusalem? Timaeus and Genesis in Counterpoint*. Ann Arbor: University of Michigan Press, 1997.

[32] Penner, T., and R. Kraut (eds.), *Nature, Knowledge and Virtue: Essays in Memory of Joan Kung (Apeiron 22)*. Edmonton: Academic Printing and Publishing, 1989.

[33] Plutarch, *De Animae Procreatione in Timaeo*, in *Plutarch's Moralia*, vol. 13, pt. 1, translated by H. Cherniss. Cambridge, Mass.: Loeb Classical Library, 1976.

[34] Pradeau, J. F., *Le Monde de la Politique*. Sankt Augustin: Academia Verlag, 1997.

[35] Prior, W. J., *Unity and Development in Plato's Metaphysics*. La Salle, Ill.: Open Court, 1985.

[36] Proclus, *In Timaeum*, edited by E. Diehl. Leipzig: Teubner, 1903.

[37] Robinson, T. M., *Plato's Psychology*. Toronto: University of Toronto Press, 1970, 1995.

[38] Sorabji, R., *Time, Creation and the Continuum*. Ithaca, N.Y.: Cornell University Press, 1983.

[39] Taylor, A. E., *A Commentary on Plato's Timaeus*. Oxford: Clarendon Press, 1928; repr. New York: Garland, 1967.

[40] Vlastos, G., *Studies in Greek Philosophy*, vol. 2, edited by D. W. Graham. Princeton: Princeton University Press, 1995.

[41] ———, *Plato's Universe*. Seattle: University of Washington Press, 1975.

[42] ——— (ed.), *Plato I. Metaphysics and Epistemology*. Garden City: Doubleday, 1971.

[43] ——— (ed.), *Plato II. Ethics, Politics and Philosophy of Art and Religion*. Garden City: Doubleday, 1971.

[44] Werkmeister, W. H. (ed.), *Facets of Plato's Philosophy*. Assen: Van Gorcum, 1976.

[45] Wilson, J. C., *On the Interpretation of Plato's* Timaeus *and On the Platonist Doctrine of the* Asymbletoi Arithmoi. London: Nutt, 1889; repr. New York: Garland, 1980.

[46] Zeyl, D. J. (ed.), *Encyclopedia of Classical Philosophy*. Westport, Ct.: Greenwood Press, 1997.

Articles:

[47] Brandwood, L., "Stylometry and Chronology," in [26], 90–120.

[48] Brown, L., "The Verb 'To Be' in Greek Philosophy: Some Remarks," in [18], 212–36.

[49] Cherniss, H. F., "The Relation of the *Timaeus* to Plato's Later Dialogues," in [1], 339–78, and [10], 298–338.

[50] ———, "A Much Misread Passage of the *Timaeus* (*Timaeus* 49c7– 50b5)," in [10], 346–63.

[51] ———, "The Sources of Evil in Plato," in [43], 244–58.

[52] ———, "*Timaeus* 52c2–5," in [10], 364–75.

[53] ———, "*Timaeus* 38a8–b5," in [10], 340–45.

[54] Dillon, J., "Tampering with the *Timaeus*: Ideological Emendations in Plato, with Special Reference to the *Timaeus*." *American Journal of Philology* 110 (1989), 50–72.

[55] Fine, G., "Owen's Progress." *Philosophical Review* 97 (1988), 373–99.

[56] Frede, D., "The Philosophical Economy of Plato's Psychology: Rationality and Common Concepts in the *Timaeus*," in [21], 29–58.

[57] Frede, M., "The Original Notion of Cause," in [19], 125–50.

[58] Gill, C., "The Genre of the Atlantis Story." *Classical Philology* 72 (1977), 287–304.

[59] ———, "Plato's Atlantis Story and the Birth of Fiction." *Philosophy and Literature* 3 (1979), 64–78.

[60] Gill, M. L., "Matter and Flux in Plato's *Timaeus*." *Phronesis* 32 (1987), 34–53.

[61] Grube, G. M. A., "The Composition of the World Soul." *Classical Philology* 27 (1932), 80–82.

[62] Gulley, N., "The Interpretation of Plato, *Timaeus* 49D–E." *American Journal of Philology* 81 (1960), 53–64.

[63] Hackforth, R., "Plato's Cosmogony." *Classical Quarterly* n.s. 9 (1959), 17–22.

[64] ———, "Plato's Theism," in [1], 439–47.

[65] Kahn, C. H., "The Greek Verb 'To Be' and the Concept of Being." *Foundations of Language* 2 (1966), 245–65.

[66] Keyt, D., "The Mad Craftsman of the *Timaeus*." *Philosophical Review* 80 (1971), 230–35.

[67] Kraut, R., "Introduction to the Study of Plato," in [26], 1–50.

[68] ———, "Plato," in [46], 387–413.

[69] Kung, J., "Mathematics and Virtue in Plato's *Timaeus*," in [3], 309–39.

[70] Lee, E. N., "Reason and Rotation: Circular Movement as the Model of Mind (*Nous*) in the Later Plato," in [44], 70–102.

[71] ———, "On the Gold-Example in Plato's *Timaeus* (50A5–B5)," in [2], 219–35.

[72] ———, "On Plato's *Timaeus* 49d4–e7." *American Journal of Philology* 88 (1967), 1–28.

[73] ———, "On the Metaphysics of the Image in Plato's *Timaeus*." *Monist* 50 (1966), 341–68.

[74] Mills, K. W., "Some Aspects of Plato's Theory of Forms: *Timaeus* 49c ff." *Phronesis* 13 (1968), 145–70.

[75] Mohr, R., "Image, Flux and Space in Plato's *Timaeus*." *Phoenix* 34 (1980), 138–52.

[76] Morrow, G. R., "Necessity and Persuasion in Plato's *Timaeus*," in [1], 421–38.

[77] Mueller, I., "Joan Kung's Reading of Plato's *Timaeus*," in [32], 1–27.

[78] Osborne, C., "Space, Time, Shape, and Direction: Creative Discourse in the *Timaeus*," in [22], 179–211.

[79] Owen, G. E. L., "Plato on Not-Being," in [42], 223–67 and [29], 104–37.

[80] ———, "Plato and Parmenides on the Timeless Present," *Monist* 50 (1966), 317–40 and [29], 27–44.

[81] ———, "The Place of the *Timaeus* in Plato's Dialogues," in [1], 313–38, and [29], 65–84.

[82] Parry, R. D., "The Intelligible World-Animal in Plato's *Timaeus*." *Journal of the History of Philosophy* 29 (1991), 13–32.

[83] ———, "The Unique World of the *Timaeus*." *Journal of the History of Philosophy* 17 (1979), 1–10.

[84] Patterson, R., "The Unique Worlds of the *Timaeus*." *Phoenix* 35 (1981), 105–19.

[85] Perl, E. D., "The Demiurge and the Forms: A Return to the Ancient Interpretation of Plato's *Timaeus*." *Ancient Philosophy* 18 (1998), 81–92.

[86] Phillips, J. F., "NeoPlatonic Exegeses of Plato's Cosmology." *Journal of the History of Philosophy* 35 (1997) 173–97.

[87] Popper, K. R., "Plato, *Timaeus* 54e–55a." *Classical Review* 20 (1970), 4–5.

[88] Pritchard, Paul, "The Meaning of *Dynamis* at Timaeus 31c." *Phronesis* 35 (1990), 182–93.

[89] Robinson, T. M., "Understanding the *Timaeus*," in [12], 103–19.

[90] ———, "Quattro note sulla cosmo-teologia di Platone." *Discorsi* 1 (1982), 113–20.

[91] ———, "The Argument of *Timaeus* 27d ff." *Phronesis* 24 (1979), 105–9.

[92] Silverman, A., "Timean Particulars." *Classical Quarterly* n.s. 42 (1992), 87–113.

[93] Strange, S. K., "The Double Explanation in the *Timaeus*." *Ancient Philosophy* 5 (1985), 25–39.

[94] Tarán, L., "The Creation Myth in Plato's *Timaeus*," in [2], 372–407.

[95] Vlastos, G., "The Disorderly Motion in the *Timaeus*," in [1], 379–99 and [40], 247–64.

[96] ———, "Creation in the *Timaeus*: Is It a Fiction?" in [1], 401–19 and [40], 265–79.

[97] ———, "Reasons and Causes in the *Phaedo*," in [42], 132–66.

[98] ———, "Was Plato a Feminist?" in [25], 115–28.

[99] Von Staden, H., "Hippocrates and the Hippocratic Corpus," in [46], 274–76.

[100] Waterlow, S., "The Third Man's Contribution to Plato's Paradeigmatism." *Mind* 91 (1982), 339–57.

[101] White, N., "Perceptual and Objective Properties in Plato," in [32] (1989), 45–65.

[102] Whittaker, J., "Textual comments on *Timaeus* 27c–d." *Phoenix* 27 (1973), 387–91.

[103] ———, "*Timaeus* 27d5 ff." *Phoenix* 23 (1969), 181–85.

[104] Young, C. M., "Plato and Computer Dating." *Oxford Studies in Ancient Philosophy* 12 (1994), 227–50.

[105] Zeyl, D. J., "Commentary of Robinson," in [12], 120–25.

[106] ———, "Plato and Talk of a World in Flux: *Timaeus* 49a6–50b5." *Harvard Studies in Classical Philology* 79 (1975), 125–48.